Sigmund Freud
**The
World
Within**

Frontispiece photograph:
Sigmund Freud and Martha Bernays, 1885.
(Courtesy of Mrs. E. L. Freud)

Sigmund Freud: The World Within

Anne E. Neimark

HARCOURT
BRACE
JOVANOVICH
New York and London

by the same author
TOUCH OF LIGHT: The Story of Louis Braille

Printed in the United States of America

Library of Congress Cataloging in Publication Data

Neimark, Anne E
Sigmund Freud: the world within.

Bibliography: p.
Includes index.
SUMMARY: A biography of the world-famous
Austrian doctor who spent his life analyzing the
mind and its illnesses.
1. Freud, Sigmund, 1856-1939—Juvenile litera-
ture. [1. Freud, Sigmund, 1856-1939.
2. Psychiatrists] I. Title.
BF173.F85N35   150'.19'52 [92]   76-18713
ISBN 0-15-274164-X

First edition

B C D E F G H I J K

To Jules Gelperin, M.D.
who held the looking-glass
with skill and patience—
and who kept it so finely
polished

Contents

I

Prophecy and Destiny

The year was 1866, in Vienna, Austria. Ten-year-old Sigmund Freud tossed in his bed in a small ghetto apartment. Shivering beneath his blanket, he sat up and blinked. What had he dreamed? It made him still afraid. Was it the train again, he asked himself, shrieking and shrilling like the cry of a demon? No, the dream was about his mother. She was being carried to her bed by strange creatures with beaks. She had looked so limp and helpless. Had she called his name?

The shivering settled down on him, and Sigmund tugged the blanket over his knees. November, in the ghetto, was always so icy and cold. When he would come home from school at the Sperl Gymnasium, he could see the glaze on the cracks of cobblestones, and the dust frozen on globes of lamps.

The winter, especially, left its mark on the ghetto. Sigmund could hardly recall the white country house in Freiberg where he and Anna had been born. His baby brother, Julius, was born in Freiberg—but had died in the country house. Mostly, Sigmund had played and fought with a nephew John, who was a year older. Sigmund had not understood why John was his nephew or why Sigmund's father was a grandfather to John.

"How can I explain such things to you?" Sigmund's mother, Amalie, would say. "When I was a girl, Sigmund, your father was already grown. He married, and the marriage brought him your half brothers, Emmanuel and Philipp. Then your father's wife died, and he came to marry me. He is a grandfather to John because John is Emmanuel's son."

The years in Freiberg were veiled in a blurred confusion. Only the tastes and smells of Freiberg's forest lingered in Sigmund's mind. He had loved to run beneath the dark archway of trees. Salamanders would wink secrets at him, and he stumbled over berries and blossoms in their fiery colors. After his father, Jakob, had told him that Freiberg no longer welcomed the Freuds—because they were Jews— Sigmund had vowed never to forget his forest.

"Why, Papa?" he'd asked. "Why aren't we welcome in Freiberg? Why must we move? Jews sit in temple and say the prayers. But you do not go to temple!"

"I am what is called a 'free-thinker,' " his father had answered. "But I am proud of our people, Sigmund, and of our ancestors before us. For centuries they've been forced to wander the earth, searching a home that could be theirs. We will search, also, in Leipzig or Vienna. And Emmanuel's family will move to England."

Leaving his bed, Sigmund tiptoed to the window and rested his face against the glass. Even in Vienna's ghetto, he had not forgotten the forest. A train had torn him from Freiberg—how he *dreaded* the trains!—and he now had five sisters and a little brother. But still he remembered the forest. He had written to John, in England, of the trees that had clustered like a cocoon at Freiberg's edge.

In the street below Sigmund's window, a straw broom was frosted with strips of ice. The dream about his mother was fading, and he was glad. By dawn, the old bearded men—the sect of the Hasidim—would gather at the curbstones, arguing in Hebrew over passages from the Torah. Then the street would fill with merchants, haggard shopkeepers, and women in drab clothes. Sigmund would watch his father carrying across the ghetto the bolts of cloth that were for sale.

In Vienna, Sigmund had learned what it meant to be a Jew. In this capital city of the Austro-Hungarian Empire, he had gazed in amazement at the Christian palaces and cathedrals, stepping along the wide ribbon of boulevards that wound beneath the carriage of the Emperor Franz Josef. His mother had told him that a peasant woman once touched his baby carriage, promising him good fortune. And his mother had said that he was born in a caul—an extra layer of skin on his head, soon snipped away, which foretold a fine future. Yet Sigmund wondered how she could believe in destiny for him, or greatness. Huddled off in the ghetto, Jewish synagogues had been destroyed, and houses crumbled toward the street. When the first emperor of the royal Hapsburg family had taken the throne, Jews were banned from study at the University of Vienna or from walking outdoors on Christian holidays or Sunday mornings.

Sigmund kneeled on the wooden floor, propping his elbows over the sill. Why, he wondered, did Jews need to wander the earth without homeland? Why was there such suffering without reason? "Men must learn to think, Sigmund," his father had said. "That is one answer to all your 'whys.' It is knowledge and understanding that are the true weapons against hate."

"Is that why you study books, Papa?" Sigmund had asked. "Is that why you read and do not send us to temple?"

"Yes," had come the reply, "that is the reason. And that is why I taught you to read, Sigmund, even before you went to school."

He remembered how he had stood before his mother, reciting Darwin and Shakespeare. "What a genius you are, Sigmund," his mother had said. "It is no wonder that prophecies were made for your future."

He turned now toward his bookshelves. Yes, books had given him comfort, also—just as they did his father. At the age of seven, he had read the whole of Thiers' *Consulate and Empire*, the story of Napoleon's rise to power. And stirred with a fearful awe, he'd found tales of other brave and mighty men—of Alexander of Macedonia, of Hannibal of Carthage, of Marshal André Masséna who was said to be a Jew. His parents had struggled to buy him more books. And when war broke out between Austria and Prussia, he'd run to South Station in Vienna, watching the wounded soldiers being carried from the trains. How triumphant to be brave! he had thought—but then, with no warning, he had retched into his scarf. Why? he'd been wondering. Why did he retch? What was the reason?

"Sigmund?" came a small whisper. "Can you read Pauli a story?"

He rose swiftly from the window, startled by the voice. In the doorway, shadowed against the hall, was his youngest sister, Pauli. "I woke up," Pauli said, clutching her slippers. "Can you read me a story?"

"Shhhh!" he answered her. "Mama and Papa are sleeping. Anna, Rosa, Mitzi, and Dolfi are sleeping. And so is the baby. You must go back to bed."

"Mama's door is shut," Pauli said. "Can you read me, Sigmund, about *Alexander*?"

Sigmund sighed. He moved to his desk, pulling a book from the shelf. Ever since he'd entered the Sperl Gymnasium, he was the storyteller for his sisters. Most of the ghetto families were large, but sometimes he imagined himself the only heir of a royal household, perhaps a prince who would be a king. In truth, he was his mother's most favored among his sisters and brother. To him, she had given a tiny room of his own in the small ghetto apartment. And to him came the precious oil lamp for his studies, while the rest of the family kept only candles.

"What have you learned already," he asked Pauli, "of Alexander the Macedonian?"

"He was very brave," Pauli whispered. "He

rode a white horse. He was a king. And when Mama said you could name our baby brother, you called him Alexander."

"Yes," Sigmund said, opening the book's tattered cover.

"Are *you* very brave, Sigmund?" Pauli asked then.

Sigmund looked down at her smooth, rounded cheeks. Might someone be brave, he wondered, yet retch at the sight of blood? Might someone be strong, but quake at the shrilling train? Often he had asked himself Pauli's question, fearing the answer but wanting to know. Now, he could hear his sister whispering dreamily, "Mama says, Sigmund, that you are very, *very* brave."

Sigmund pulled the blanket from his bed and wrapped it about Pauli's shoulders. In the hallway, he could glimpse the dark frame of his parents' door. "What does Papa say of me?" he heard himself ask, astonished at his own words.

Pauli settled herself on the rug to hear the story from Sigmund's book. "Papa does not say," she answered. But then she added, "Once, when Mama spoke of you, Papa said she was foolish. What does foolish mean, Sigmund?"

Sigmund bent toward his book, an arc of yellow lamplight pressing across the window. "It means, Pauli," he replied softly, "that I shall have to try very, very hard."

But when his sister looked puzzled, Sigmund began to read aloud from the pages, reciting to Pauli the chronicle of Alexander the Macedonian and of Bucephalus, the white steed.

When Sigmund was fourteen, Vienna was astir

with a war between France and Prussia. Jakob Freud's trade in textiles had not flourished, and small sums of money arrived from Emmanuel in England. The family lived sparsely, and Sigmund's sisters learned to sew. On the chilliest days, Sigmund would study his schoolbooks by the old porcelain stove in the kitchen, or bundle into his woolens to walk pensively among the stalls of the junk market at the corner.

Jews had, at last, been granted equal citizenship across the empire. They could study now at the university, although they were still hated and abused. Sigmund turned more and more frequently to his shelves of books. At the Sperl Gymnasium, he had become "first" or "primus" of his class, winning prizes for his compositions. Slim and somber-eyed, his dark hair no longer in curls, he explored the boundless terrain of his books as if in the deep of Freiberg's forest—searching Shakespeare, Sophocles, Dickens, Darwin, Thiers, Helmholtz, Voltaire.

"Our brother Sigmund," Anna announced one day to the others, "is the smartest of us children. That is why Mama saves for his books and why she sent away our old piano when he was disturbed by the noise."

"Will you be rich someday, Sigmund?" his sister Mitzi had asked.

"Perhaps," Sigmund had answered, his heart pounding inside his chest. But what, he had wondered, was he really to do? What *would* he become? "My books speak of learning the Truth," he'd told his sister Mitzi. "And perhaps someday I shall know what is true from what is not."

In spring weather, when a thin mist hung over

the river Danube and peddlers set out their wares on the streets, Sigmund would hike into the countryside beyond Vienna. With a book tucked into his pocket, he climbed the limestone cliffs of the Wienerwald or strolled beneath the peach and apricot trees near Kahlenberg Mountain. "You stay away so long," his mother would say, brushing the burrs from his clothes. But, smiling, he would present her with a spray of purple pasque flowers or a bundle of wild mushrooms.

Surrounded by sky and mountain, Sigmund would feel as if he'd come home. Once more, as when he was small, he could touch the tight curling of tree moss or breathe in the scent of the early heather. Secrets would whisper at him in the wind, and magic might roll in the buds of flowers. "How much there is to learn," he said to himself—for, slowly, knowledge had begun to hold as much power for him as any weapons or triumphs of war.

The child in him was growing older. He bestowed his box of toy soldiers upon his little brother, Alexander, and at school he prepared a paper entitled "Considerations Involved in the Choice of a Profession." From England, Emmanuel offered to make a place for him in business, and his mother had managed to borrow enough money from relatives to send him on to the university. But what, he kept prodding himself, would he study for his future? Unlike many of his classmates, he did not want to choose business or law. And as for being a doctor of medicine, though he no longer retched at the sight of wounds or blood, he wished more to *discover* than to cure.

Shortly before his graduation, Sigmund heard

the recitation of an essay on nature. The words of that essay, written by the German poet Wolfgang von Goethe, were to lead Sigmund toward enrolling in the program of natural science at Vienna's university. Goethe's essay rang with a love of nature and with a reverence for beauty. And while Sigmund hearkened to the memory of his beloved forest—to the flowing trees and the distant meadows—the thought of science suddenly thrilled.

All across Europe, natural science had become a respected department of study. Even in the coffee houses of Vienna, there was talk of Darwin's theories on evolution and of Helmholtz's writings on the conservation of energy. Through science, Sigmund had told himself, might come the pursuit of knowledge. In science was Truth.

Anxiously, he hoped to convince his father of his decision, to win Jakob's approval and support. A university tuition would place further burdens upon the family, and as a Jew in science, he might find little chance for advancement. But Jakob, weary from his failing business, had only sighed and glanced away. "The choice is yours," Jakob had said.

Turning then to his mother, Sigmund had asked, "And what, Mama, do *you* think?"

That spring of 1873 had been lapsing into the dry and dusty days of the summer. Amalie Freud's few potato plants had wilted on their ledge above the street, and her apron was frayed from too much patching. But her face flushed with conviction. Hadn't her Sigmund been born in a *caul*, in a crown of blessings upon his head? Didn't he have the sign of a genius?

Amalie was eager to grant him whatever she could. Reaching out for her dark-haired, eldest son, she had nodded proudly. "I think, Sigmund," she'd answered, and as she would say in many days to come, "that you shall be the best—and the very finest—scientist in *all* of Vienna."

II

Two Roads

The door to the Institute of Physiology clattered shut on its rusty hinges. With his coattails flapping behind him, Sigmund had dashed across the square that held both the university and the Votivkirche, one of the city's most splendid churches. For the first time, he would be late for the morning lecture by Herr Professor Brücke. But he had stopped to pay on his debt at the bookstore, and the minutes had slipped away.

At the lecture room, his chair stood vacant in a nest of heads. Breathlessly, Sigmund hurried across the floor, nodding at Ernst Fleischl and Sigmund Exner, Professor Brücke's two assistants. His footsteps, however, echoed against the gray walls, and his palms grew damp under the Professor's icy stare. "Excuse me, Herr Professor," Sigmund murmured over his books. "I regret that I am late."

"Fertig! Sit down, Freud," came the reply, and the cold blue eyes pierced like knives. It was said at the institute that a scowl from the Professor could freeze the waters of the Danube. Hastily, Sigmund slid into his chair and opened his notebook. He could read now in six languages besides German and rarely needed to take notes, but he leaned over the pages in order to straighten his tie, hoping that his beard was neatly trimmed.

When he'd first entered the university, Sigmund had roamed the various departments of science. His zoology professor had sent him twice to Trieste to prepare a paper on eels, and other instructors spoke of his amazing memory and of his ability with words. Yet it was Herr Professor Brücke, the brilliant Prussian scientist, who had drawn Sigmund to physiology. At the institute, among the specimens of rabbits, fishes, and frogs, was the dark mystery of the nervous system—and the challenge of exploring nature in nerve tracts and cells. Professor Brücke believed that living creatures behaved as they did because of masses of energy currents. Even the human brain, said the Professor, could function only from waves of energy and excitement.

While his classmates graduated as doctors, Sigmund had stayed on at the university. Attending classes in the Medical College, he too had gained enough credits for a medical degree, but he ignored the examinations. Professor Brücke had offered him a part-time position as a research scholar, and although the job paid him no salary, Sigmund worked feverishly at the lab. In medicine, he wrote his nephew John in England, the body might be dissected or healed. But in science, *beguiling science*, one

could search out the very secrets of the life force
itself.

At home, Jakob had developed poor eyesight,
and Amalie was weakened from a cough. Yet the
money for the university was borrowed each year,
and little was said of the matter. "A *scientist*?" some
of Sigmund's friends would tease. "Aren't you the
Jewish son from the ghetto? How can you earn a
living, Sigmund, treating frogs and fishes instead of
people?"

After the morning lecture, Sigmund opened the
laboratory cubicle where he kept his microscope and
his slides. Ernst Fleischl, the assistant, brought him
a new batch of crayfish specimens from the shed in
the courtyard. "I'm sorry to be late this morning,"
Sigmund said to Fleischl. "If I hadn't scraped together a payment for the bookshop, they would
have closed my account."

"Don't worry, Sigmund," Fleischl answered
kindly. "When Professor Brücke thinks you're out of
hearing, he praises your work on the nerve cells.
He speaks of vital contributions by *Herr Freud*, the
scholar."

Sigmund fastened a slide, preserved with his
own formula of glycerine and nitric acid, onto the
flat stage of the microscope. Peering down through
the eyepiece, he wondered if any of his research
might bring him a promotion at the lab. Could he
hope to become an assistant like Fleischl and earn a
salary for his work? In Vienna, beneath the glitter of
the cathedrals, was a rigid moral and social structure. Rumors had flown that Sigmund Freud was
despised by the Ministry of Education because he
was a Jew. Yet several of his reports had been pub-

lished in the *Bulletin* of the Academy of Sciences. And in his paper on the Petromyzon, a primitive fish, he alone had closed a gap long argued among scientists—proving that cells in the nervous systems of lower animals were similar to those in higher forms of life.

Throughout the remainder of the morning, Sigmund worked in the lab. By afternoon, he'd left to attend seminars at the university in physics and anatomy, walking home before twilight across the inner city and toward the boundaries of the ghetto. A soft wind soothed the tension in his head, and he stretched out his coat sleeves to cover the glycerine stains on his cuffs. At the old wooden bridge that spanned the Danube canal, he paused to glance down at the splintered pilings. Ripples of blue and amber—as blue as Professor Brücke's eyes—lapped lazily beneath him, and a train whistle moaned in the distance.

A train. . . . Suddenly, the train sounds whirled against Sigmund's ears, and he was clutched by a spasm of dizziness. Anxiously, he waited for the thundering roar to drift away. Yet even as the wheels sped off into a haze that floated over the Danube, Sigmund clung tightly to the wooden bridge.

"Again?" he asked himself grimly. Nightmares still rose to torment him, and headaches or dizziness would come and go. How long would the train sounds upset him? He'd been told that on the express from Freiberg, he'd screamed at the sight of gas jets flaring up from the station platform. But that childhood train ride was far behind him. Why should events from the *past*, from what was finished and done, be affecting him now?

Staring downward into the water, Sigmund moved slowly across the bridge. Almost four years before he'd been sent on a brief vacation to England, and he'd trembled at the sounds of the train. Perhaps, he thought gloomily, there was some injury to his own brain cells, as in the malformed specimens at the lab. Why else, when his health appeared excellent, should he suffer such feelings? In seminars, he'd been taught that for every physical sensation there was a physical cause, that for every pain or discomfort of the body, there was some injury, lesion, malformation, or disease. Yet what, he questioned as he walked dizzily onto the street, did his own symptoms mean?

In the summers of 1879 and 1880, Sigmund studied the nerve cells of the crayfish. Using one of the most difficult lenses on the microscope, he made the discovery that the nerve fiber, which other scientists had seen as a column of liquid, was actually composed of tissue. His research would be an important contribution to neurology, the science of nerve cells and their function. By isolating the unit of nerve fiber and cell, Sigmund had come close to describing the "neurone theory," which is taught today in classes of physiology.

Between the months of his summer research, he was assigned to military duty in the army. The empire, however, was not at war, and he was sent to stand about in the corridors of a Viennese hospital. Lonely for the laboratory, he kept himself busy through an outside assignment for an editor, translating a book of essays by the British author John Stuart Mill.

But when he returned to the university, Sigmund was not promoted from his post. A Jew, he was informed, should not expect to become an assistant. He cut his expenses down to the barest essentials and ate only two meals a day—yet it seemed impossible to keep himself in science. Guiltily, he borrowed from Fleischl at the lab and from a friend, Dr. Josef Breuer. When he could not afford a birthday gift for his sister Rosa, he finally forced himself to take his *rigorosa,* the examinations in medicine. Eight years had passed since he'd entered the university. What other choice did he have but to be a doctor? His interests were tied to science, but if he did not wish to starve himself and his family, he would have to practice medicine. He would need to train for several years in medical service.

"*So!*" Amalie had declared. "You will be as fine a doctor, Sigmund, as you are a scientist. Already the neighbors stop me at the poultry shop. They have seen your name in journals. They do not understand your words, but they read the printing of your name."

"I wish the Ministry of Education," he'd told her, "felt as positive toward me, Mama, as you do."

On March 31, 1881, at the age of twenty-five, Sigmund was awarded his degree as a doctor. He would intern at Vienna's General Hospital, but he delayed leaving the institute and avoided walking past the broad cream-colored buildings that housed Vienna's sick. Three or four times more, he borrowed money from Josef Breuer in order to stay at the lab. Josef was a successful physician who conducted experiments in physiology. Often Sigmund had been invited to dine with the Breuer family or to ride along with Josef on medical calls so that the two men could talk together of philosophy, literature, or science.

One evening he was asked by Josef to travel on calls to the area of Baden. A carriage had been hired, equipped with two horses, and it sped Sigmund and Josef out of Vienna into the green spinneys and hills. "Well, Sigmund," Josef had said with a smile. "The *rigorosa* is finished. You carry the title of *Herr Doktor Freud*. A respectable accomplishment, no?"

"It is not what I intended," Sigmund answered his friend.

"But I have offered you more funds," Josef said, "to remain at the institute. You should not be ashamed, Sigmund, to take them. I invest in your talent—in what you discover for science."

Longingly, Sigmund had gazed from the carriage toward a dark strand of woods. Although he was removed from his childhood, his legs ached even now to run among the trees—to taste the forest, to seek nature's answers, *to find out* and *to know.* "I am grateful, Josef," he replied, "but I have learned that I cannot do just as I please. I have kept a ledger of what I owe you. When I leave the institute for the General Hospital, I will plan to pay back every gulden I've borrowed."

Josef sighed and tapped the medical bag that rested between them on the seat. "Do what you must," he said. "A medical practice can provide you with a decent living. But believe me, Sigmund, you will never completely abandon science. You will find the road for return."

At their destination in Baden, Josef knocked on

the door of a small stone-covered cottage. A blond child in pigtails escorted Sigmund and Josef inside, leading them to an ashen-faced man on a quilted bed. Josef rinsed his hands in a flowered bowl, and then Sigmund watched while the dressings were changed on the man's body. "This patient was injured in a boating accident," Josef explained.

Standing at the foot of the patient's bed, Sigmund could not help but notice the trust and respect that were tendered to Josef Breuer. Skillfully, as if at a loom, Josef's fingers wove the white strips of linen bandage about the man's chest and shoulders, wrapping in a gentle and easy rhythm.

"*Danke,*" the patient mumbled. "Thank you, thank you, Herr Doktor Breuer."

Catching sight, then, of his own reflection in a dresser mirror, Sigmund felt oddly withdrawn from the face in the glass. He saw the black curve of his pointed beard, the intense glow of his eyes. "But who are you?" he wanted to ask the reflection, to ask himself. "What has made you what you are? Must you leave your post in science? Can you ever be at ease with the title of doctor? Have you anything of worth to give to the sick?"

He stood quietly, confused and unsure in the cottage of Josef's patient. He had chosen a path in science that seemed no longer fair to pursue—not if he cared for the welfare of his family. He must move on, must begin anew. Was that not the fate of his ancestors and of most Jews who were not free?

"Come, Sigmund," Josef was saying to him. "Are you ready to travel home?"

"Yes," Sigmund answered, turning from the

quilted bed. But even in his uncertainty, he realized that—just as his mother had said—he *had* contributed to science. His discoveries from the laboratory would not be forgotten. His name had been marked in books and in journals.

Perhaps, he told himself, it was true that he would never completely abandon science. Perhaps he *would* find the means for return. Yet as he walked, on that evening, from the stone-covered cottage in Baden, Sigmund had not the slightest premonition that he would one day give more to the world—to man's knowledge of inner man—than even his mother might guess.

III

Dark Continent

In the summer of 1882, over a year after he had received his medical degree, Sigmund resigned from the Institute of Physiology. Professor Brücke was saddened to lose him, but Sigmund would not be missed by the Christian board of the Ministry of Education.

His last weeks in the laboratory were painfully spent. Even the slimiest specimens from the courtyard shed felt like silk to his fingers, and the microscope gleamed like precious onyx from the bench. Walking from the institute down Währinger Strasse, Sigmund would count the number of days left to him in the lab—the moments when he and Fleischl might study the spinal cord of a fish or prepare the tissue slices across a slide.

At home, he would greet the family and eat his supper in solitude. Burning the oil lamp at his desk, he would balance a dinner plate over his knees and open a textbook in his lap. "You're not ill, Sigmund, are you?" his mother might ask. "You don't eat a proper supper. You look much too thin."

"I'm fine, Mama," he would answer. "I would like Josef Breuer to check over your cough. It is *you* who look too thin."

In July he would enroll at Vienna's General Hospital. Joining the ranks of other interns, Sigmund would gain the experience of treating patients. Surrounded by rows of beds in the dusty wards, he would memorize symptoms and observe disease. He would dispense injections from wooden trays and order the rounds of medication.

He would not be as uncomfortable as he had thought. Somehow, he possessed a keen sense of disease. With the briefest outline of symptoms, he could solve the puzzle of diagnosis. His internship was a step toward his independence and self-support. And it was a step that he now took with a sudden and added incentive.

On an afternoon in April, 1882, in the parlor of his parents' shabby ghetto apartment, Sigmund had met a young woman named Martha Bernays. Twenty-one-year-old Martha was five years younger than Sigmund and the sister of Eli Bernays, an old friend of the Freuds. The Bernays family had lived in Hamburg, Germany. After the death of Martha's father, however, they had moved to Vienna.

"Good afternoon, Herr Doktor Freud," Martha had called from the parlor, her fingers gracefully peeling an apple.

The young fräulein with the slender figure and gentle manner would imprint herself at once upon Sigmund's mind. Burdened by debts, he had certainly not planned on romance—yet it was romance that seized him as surely as had his old dizziness and fears. Tossing caution aside, he began to court Martha Bernays. The few coins in his pockets were spent, each morning, on a single red rose, sent to Fräulein Martha Bernays with a small proverb or poem.

In a matter of weeks, Sigmund had invited Martha on languid strolls through Vienna's gardens, chaperoned by her sister Minna. "Before we met," he told her in a suburban garden in nearby Mödling, "work and study were all I'd planned for."

"And now," she had asked him in her soft, precise German, "your plans are to be changed?"

"Yes, Martha," he'd answered. "My plans seem to include someone who is very dear."

By mid-June, the couple was secretly engaged. Marriage, of course, would have to wait several years, until Sigmund could leave the hospital to set up medical practice. But he was able to turn more surely toward medicine and to dream of the future. "Science has meant so much to you," Martha said to him. "Can you be content, Sigmund, as a doctor? Or with me as a wife? Might you have too many regrets?"

"My future has been already marked," Sigmund answered. "I've known, for some time, that I must train at the hospital. But *you*, Martha—can you wait for *me* without too many regrets?"

Smiling the gentleness of her smile, Martha had slipped her hand into his. "I wait willingly," she told him. "You've quoted to me, Herr Doktor, from your proverbs and poems. Wasn't it the Greek poet Menander who said, 'We live not as we wish—but as we can'?"

The calm of the young woman beside him had eased his mind of worry, as it would for all the rest of his days. Sigmund promised himself that he would practice medicine as a reliable doctor. He would commit himself to the profession that he'd found it necessary to choose. And then, he thought firmly—with just a little good fortune and in spite of Menander's words—he and Martha Bernays might live *quite* as they wished.

The twelve buildings of the General Hospital, Vienna's Allgemaine Krankenhaus, encircled a four-story "Fools' Tower" where the insane were once chained. Now the tower was empty, and the hospital buildings contained all of the patients. On July 31, 1882, Sigmund signed on as an intern in the department of Surgery, moving several months later to Internal Medicine, and to Dermatology. Doctors could remain as long as they liked in any department. And Sigmund's early nerve research under Professor Brücke was to lead him to more permanent service in the department of Psychiatry and in the wards for Nervous Disease.

The psychiatry of the 1800s was mainly a listing and classifying of mental disorders. Crowded into the hospital's gloomy wards were the most miserable of the mentally ill—men and women who had set fire to their own bodies, who "heard" voices and "saw" visions, who tore out their eyelashes or screamed in strange tongues of terror and rage. The illnesses of such patients were said to arise from some physical wrong inside the body. Yet doctors had not been able to pinpoint the cause. And even among patients who died, the dissection of bodily organs might not show any sign of malfunction or disease.

"Insanity is hopeless," the doctors would say. "It is passed down among families who are unfit to survive. We cannot cure insanity. We can only lock up the insane."

In his off-duty hours in the darkened and clammy wards, Sigmund would often stop by the bedsides of mental patients. Certain disorders, he'd learned, could be easily understood. Accidents might have injured the brain or alcoholism affected the senses. In other cases, tumors could distort behavior. But some patients appeared in excellent health. Why, Sigmund would wonder, had these patients fallen ill? What had happened in the cells of their brains? What of the *hysterics*—only women were classified as such—who sank into paralytic fits, but whose diseases were invisible under a microscope? And what of the *neurotics*, who were struck by overpowering fears—fears of high places, fears of low places, fears of thunderstorms or crowds? Wouldn't Sigmund's own terror of the trains fit the category of a neurosis? Doctors might laugh at the nervously ill, but Sigmund knew the agony of such terrible feelings.

"I am blind!" one patient screamed to Sigmund in the wards, yet while she stared blankly into space, the patient's eyes were physically sound. And another woman, a Fräulein Wagner, could not bend her legs or walk—yet her muscles, nerves, and tendons were perfectly formed.

Sigmund breathed a sigh of relief that his Martha Bernays was healthy and strong. After she'd agreed to marry him, Martha had been taken by her mother for a summer in Wandsbek, Germany, but at least she would return to him. Writing long letters to Wandsbek, Sigmund had described his hours of training in the wards. And he wrote of the news of his family—his sister Mitzi's work as a nursemaid, his brother Alexander's interest in transportation, his mother's improving cough.

On many evenings, Sigmund would eat supper at Josef's apartment, where the talk would still flow as richly as Frau Breuer's sauces and creams. "You've treated the nervously ill," Sigmund said one night to his friend. "Is there no cure, Josef, for this suffering?"

"Nervous disease is our dark continent," Josef had replied. "I have notes on a patient whom I call Anna O. She suffered from hysteria, Sigmund, and would rip the buttons off her nightclothes. But this young woman managed her own treatment. If she sank into a trance, she would speak to me of her symptoms—and quickly feel improved. 'Chimney sweeping,' she called the treatment. Her 'talking cure.'"

"But how fascinating!" Sigmund said in excitement. "Tell me more, Josef! May I see your notes? How is the patient now?"

Josef, however, had abruptly ended the conversation. Talking of the case seemed oddly to distress him and to leave his wife, Mathilde, suddenly pale.

As Sigmund trained in the Psychiatric Clinic, he

was appointed to the rank of *Sekundararzt,* a kind of assistant on staff. The prejudice toward Jews was less harsh at the General Hospital than it had been at the university. Sigmund was looked upon now with increasing respect. At the bedside of a dying boy, he was asked to consult with a group of bewildered doctors. The illness of the dying boy could not be diagnosed. Sigmund had recorded the symptoms of soft, bleeding gums and of masses of black and blue marks beneath the skin. "This boy has scurvy," Sigmund had said. "We will find, however, the destruction of certain tissue within the brain. The more critical diagnosis is *scorbutic cerebral hemorrhage."*

The doctors seemed doubtful at this rare diagnosis, for the symptoms were so few. But when the unfortunate boy had died and his body was sent for autopsy, their doubts disappeared. Carefully, with widening eyes, the pathologist had lifted up the sick and discolored tissue from the boy's brain. "Yes," the pathologist had said. "Scorbutic cerebral hemorrhage."

On another occasion, after a paper of Sigmund's was printed in the *Medical Weekly,* he was called to the bedside of a young baker. The baker was in severe pain, with a chill shuddering through his body. Tests had ruled out every disease from tuberculosis to meningitis, but Sigmund had leaned over the young man's bed. Running his fingers over the tightened stomach muscles, he had seen them ripple and stretch. And tapping the reflexes on the patient's leg, he had watched the intensity of the response. *"Acute polyneuritis*—an inflammation of nerves throughout the body," Sigmund had announced, in a diagnosis never before made in Vienna.

Again, because no cure was possible, the patient had died. And once more, Sigmund was proven correct when the pathologist had removed the pulpy networks of diseased and inflamed nerves.

Sigmund was asked, then, to teach a small class to interns at the hospital, lecturing on the diagnosis of brain disorders. He was pleased and surprised—as were Martha and his family—but in accepting the appointment, he was not willing to ignore those mental diseases that seemed to have no cause or cure. He spoke to his class of hysteria and neurosis. The specialty of Nervous Disease—of treating the mentally ill—was, indeed, a continent in utter darkness.

Sigmund remembered Anna O., the patient of Josef's who had "talked away" her own symptoms. He was intrigued at the thought of exploring such a case. So many lives were being wasted in mental disease, lives that should be lived. Some sense must be made of all the misery—of the unexplained tics, tremors, and paralyses, of the baffling failures of vision and hearing, of the "incurable" delusions of minds said to be insane.

For Sigmund, a mission was undeniably taking root. In May of 1883—between his mother's tears and pride and his father's awkward handshake—he had moved from the family apartment to a room at the General Hospital. He was contributing more and more hours in the wards for Nervous Disease.

Martha was again away, visiting in Hamburg, but he explained to her in a letter that neurologists and psychiatrists were extremely scarce in Vienna. Too many doctors were repulsed or discouraged by the mentally ill. But if Martha would wait a while longer, Sigmund had written, they could share the future together, in all its demands.

A letter had arrived in Vienna from Hamburg. *"I will wait,"* Martha had said.

Sigmund was touching now upon a well of strength deep within him. His sense of a place for himself had grown as he'd walked the wards of the General Hospital. He was not to be swept aside by either ghetto or poverty, by burden or task. What must be endured, he would endure—since only the foolish would not rejoice in challenge or struggle.

A man's work, he thought, was a blessing. Challenges were a spur. Weren't even the darkest of forests and continents made to be explored?

IV

Look, Look, and Look Again

During the four and a half years of their engagement, Sigmund wrote more than nine hundred letters to Martha Bernays. Martha's mother was not at all pleased with the romance and had moved her daughter to Hamburg, but the letters poured onward. Sigmund watched his sister Anna being wed to Martha's brother, Eli, and he tolerated advice from friends that he should pick a wealthier girl for his lifemate and bride. He paid the advice, however, no heed.

At moments he believed that he might gain enough recognition for early riches and fame. With a microscope in the hospital's Psychiatric Clinic— encouraged by the chief brain anatomist Dr. Theodor Meynert—Sigmund developed a method of staining brain tissue so that the fibers were bright and clear. His method was printed in a Viennese journal and translated into English for the publication *Brain*. Yet the discovery brought him no money, and although doctors in training were allowed private patients, Sigmund treated only a few cases that were sent to him from Josef Breuer.

His greater hope for recognition beyond Vienna had lain in a drug called cocaine. Made from the leaves of the coca tree, cocaine powder was swallowed for energy by South American Indians. No one had bothered to investigate cocaine—nor were there many laws about testing or selling drugs—so in the best tradition of his times, Sigmund had tested out cocaine by swallowing small amounts himself.

He discovered that the powder could immediately lift the spirits. His headaches and dizziness were magically gone, and the drug did not seem to leave complications. Sigmund tested cocaine further, finding that it numbed pain throughout the body. He recommended bits of the powder to Martha, to bring the "roses" into her cheeks, and he spoke of it to Ernst Fleischl who suffered now from infected tumors across one hand. Fleischl had become addicted to another drug, morphine, but he reported that he felt better with cocaine than he had in months.

Finding more and more uses for this seemingly harmless drug—it settled stomach distress, it helped digestion—Sigmund prepared a short paper on cocaine and had it published in Vienna. Almost at once, physicians wrote for information from around the world. Drug companies in Europe and America invited Sigmund to conduct experiments on cocaine and to lecture before medical audiences.

He sent off rapturous letters to Martha. If his hopes for riches came true, he told her, the two of them could be married far earlier than they'd dreamed.

Yet life was not to be easy, and a sobering lesson would be learned. Gradually, after cocaine had been used on hundreds of patients, reports crept in of some addiction—of fits of trembling and even of death. Small amounts of the powder might be helpful and safe, but larger doses could cause disaster.

At first, Sigmund tried to defend cocaine. To his horror, however, he heard that Fleischl had been buying a constant supply and was hopelessly addicted. Fainting spells had developed, and ghastly hallucinations. In shame, spending night after night caring for his friend, Sigmund began receiving letters that accused him of unleashing a "scourge" upon mankind. He spoke no further of cocaine— and by the time the drug was hailed as a successful pain-killer in eye operations, it was the eye surgeon Carl Koller who won early fame and riches—even though Sigmund himself had suggested cocaine.

"It is terribly hard," Sigmund wrote to Martha in Germany. "Do you realize that all happiness is hemmed in by limitations which one only has to think of in order to become very unhappy? Let us cling to one another all the closer . . ."

And, later, he asked, "Do you think you can continue to love me if things go on like this for years; I buried in work and struggling for elusive success, and you lonely and far away? I think you will have to, Marty, and in return I shall love you very much."

Sigmund's pleasures, if he was not working at

the hospital, were taken mainly in his books, his family, his letters to Martha, and in nature. Never had he tired of his hikes across the cliffs of the Wienerwald or beneath the rise of Kahlenberg Mountain. Once or twice a week, having at last told his parents of his engagement, he would join them for supper. Slipping after the meal into the tiled kitchen, he would leave whatever coins he could spare from his hospital salary in a bowl on the table.

"You must rest, Papa," he would say to his father. "You and Mama must not worry about what is ahead."

"I've forgotten, Sigmund," Jakob had answered, "what it is not to worry."

Amalie had grown stouter, and was no longer young, but her faith in her son's destiny had been unruffled. "Ah, Sigmund," Amalie would say, "I scarcely mind sharing you with Martha. You shall be the salvation of us all."

On the shelves in his hospital room, Sigmund's collection of books had slowly mounted over the years. He would send a few copies to Martha, wanting her to share his thrill in *David Copperfield* by Dickens or in Cervantes' *Don Quixote*. Occasionally, he permitted himself a back seat at the theater, where he might enjoy Shakespearean drama or the play by Sophocles *Oedipus Rex*. The tragedy of Oedipus—who had murdered his own father and married his mother—stirred in Sigmund some chord of response. Long after the final curtain, he would relive the stunning production of *Oedipus*, searching for meaning in content or theme.

In 1885, Sigmund applied at the General Hospital for the rank of *privatdocent*. The title did not carry a salary, but it allowed a doctor to present lectures at the university. By now, Sigmund had written nine clinical papers. His reputation, in spite of the paper on cocaine, would win him the title— and also a special travel grant of 600 gulden. With the substantial grant, he might study outside of Vienna in the field of Nervous Disease. He would be sent to Paris, France, to train for six months under the guidance of the famous neurologist Jean Martin Charcot. And he would acquire the final experience needed to complete his hospital service and to open a reputable practice in the treatment of Nervous Disease.

At the Institute of Physiology, Sigmund thanked his old professor Ernst Brücke, who had persuaded the hospital to award him the grant. And to Martha, whom he planned to visit in Hamburg, he wrote excitedly, ". . . my little Princess . . . I am coming with money and . . . [I will] go on to Paris and become a great scholar . . . and then we will soon get married, and I will cure all the incurable nervous cases and through you I shall be healthy . . ."

On the last day of August, 1885, Sigmund gave up his hospital quarters and prepared to travel to Hamburg. Joyously, he spent several days visiting Martha, and then again had to bid her good-bye. He was determined not to be terrorized by the thunder of the trains, and although his knees shook as he descended onto the platform in Paris, he asked directions to his hotel and walked the route by himself.

Around him, he could feel the lightheartedness of the city. Spacious boulevards swung away from the banks of the river Seine, and music played in the parks. Children were pulled in goat-drawn carts, and teen-agers frolicked in front of him, holding hands without shame.

Although Sigmund longed for the closeness of Martha, he did not miss Vienna. He was aware that Paris was a city of beauty and laughter. Each day, he walked from his hotel to the Salpêtrière, the charity hospital where Jean Martin Charcot treated Nervous Disease. The Salpêtrière had served as an asylum for the insane, its inmates starved, chained, and beaten to "free" them of "demons." Only the compassion of a French doctor, Philippe Pinel, had put an end to the brutal treatment.

Sigmund was fascinated by the work of Jean Martin Charcot. The man himself was overpowering, thin wisps of hair tucked behind his ears, eyes probing yet soft. Charcot would stalk through the wards of the Salpêtrière, calling out or naming diseases of the nerves. "*Paralysis agitans,* a trembling of the body," Charcot would exclaim. "*Multiple sclerosis, cerebro-spinal sclerosis, epilepsy, meningitis.*"

Charcot's interest had focused on female hysteria, the disease he believed was caused from an undiscovered brain injury or lesion. But hysteria, he insisted, could occur in *males* as well as in females. Men also might be afflicted with limbs that had gone strangely numb, with hearts that beat too rapidly, with throats that would not swallow.

"If the symptoms exist," Charcot had said, "the illness is real. Hysteria may copy the symptoms of paralysis—though the copy is far from exact—but it is an actual disorder."

At the Salpêtrière, Charcot did not rely on

syrups or electric massage to ease his patients. As a man acclaimed for boldness, Charcot had dared to use hypnotism to treat hysteria. Hypnosis, a trance-like state in which a person responds to commands, was first introduced by a Dr. Franz Mesmer. The method was called Mesmerism, but doctors had regarded it as dangerous trickery. In the 1840s, however, an Englishman named James Braid described the method as scientific, renaming it hypnotism.

Poised dramatically before a group of students and visiting doctors, Jean Martin Charcot would demonstrate on a hysterical patient. Sigmund watched in rapt attention while Charcot held on to a trembling young woman. The woman could not raise her left arm, and her head jerked spasmodically to the side. Speaking softly, Charcot had said to the patient, "You are feeling tired, Mademoiselle Weil. You are *very* tired. Your eyes are growing heavy. You will hear my voice and obey me. You will sleep. You will sleep."

In moments, the young woman had swooned backward against Charcot's shoulder. Being susceptible to hypnotism, claimed Charcot, was in itself a disease. But Sigmund wondered whether hypnotism had simply reached into some secret part of the mind, as if it bypassed the usual patterns of thought. If that were so, however, *why* was the mind able to affect the body? Hadn't Sigmund been taught that body and mind were *separate*, that thoughts had no connection to physical feelings?

"Now, Mademoiselle Weil," Charcot had commanded his patient. "Raise your paralyzed arm! Raise your arm, Mademoiselle Weil! Raise it above your waist!" And slowly, against a gasp from the astonished audience, the young woman's paralyzed arm had lifted upward. *"Bien!* Good!" Charcot exclaimed. "Now, Mademoiselle, your head will stop jerking. Can you hear me? Your head will rest normally. It will rest as it should."

And, amazingly, the poor woman's spasm slowed to a halt—until one more command released her from the trance of hypnosis.

Sigmund wrote home of Charcot that "no other human being has ever affected me in the same way." Charcot had given Sigmund permission to translate some studies into German, a rare privilege for an unknown doctor from Vienna. Fresh from early morning visits to the church of Notre Dame or to the Louvre Museum, Sigmund would watch Charcot not only removing symptoms under hypnosis—but producing them as well. He listened to Charcot advise that one must "look, look, and look again" in order to see the truth. And struck by the mysterious power of thought, by the *mind*, Sigmund once more pondered the "talking cure" of Anna O. He spoke of the case at the Salpêtrière, but Charcot did not express interest.

In February of 1886, Sigmund left Paris to visit a children's neurology clinic in Berlin. He had completed his training under the grant and would return to Vienna to open treatment in Nervous Disease. The money from the grant had dwindled away, and there would be little income from his first year of practice. But a doctor at the General Hospital insisted on giving him a gift of extra funds. "A new era is beginning," he wrote to Martha in Germany. "A good one I hope, one that will bring good things."

Sigmund's first consultation with a patient was held after he had rented two large rooms in an apartment house near Vienna's Town Hall. One room was divided by a curtain to make a bedroom, leaving space for both an office and study. Furnishings were provided, and few utensils would be needed. Mathilde Breuer, Josef's wife, had designed two plaques with Sigmund's name on them, to be attached to the building at the street entrance and the inside doorway. Sigmund mounted the glass and porcelain plaques himself, nailing them into the stone blocks and wood.

It was the afternoon before Easter, 1886, when he stood silently on the pavement to survey the glass plaque at the entrance. Grandly, it announced his title: *Privatdocent Dr. Sigmund Freud.* Sigmund breathed in the cool air of that April. It was the month of his first meeting, four years before, with Martha Bernays. Suddenly, it seemed ridiculous to him to wait much longer for marriage. Martha was far away in Germany, and he wanted her with him. If she were well and happy, he did not care if he himself ate only *one* meal a day. He would summon Martha to him, and she would come to be his bride.

No one noticed the thin, dark-haired man in the street as he paced before the stone wall. Sigmund knew that he had no guarantees, either, of being noticed in private practice—of having enough patients ask for a young Jewish doctor who hoped to treat the untreatable in Nervous Disease. But his experiences in Paris had opened him to bolder ideas. Science and medicine might possibly be welded.

There could be cures and treatments that no one had dared try—not even the world-famous neurologist Jean Martin Charcot. As he thought of Charcot, Sigmund recalled a line from *Hamlet*, the Shakespearean drama. "There are more things in heaven and earth, Horatio," Hamlet had said, "than are dreamt of in your philosophy." The splendor of those prophetic words caroled like bells within Sigmund's mind.

V

Mind and Body

A new building rose, on the street called Maria Theresienstrasse, among the old, ornate apartment houses with their faded facades. The new building stood on the site where four hundred people had lost their lives in a fire at the Viennese State Theater. Most families shunned the new apartments, fearing the taint of death—but it was here that Sigmund and Martha moved after their marriage on September 13, 1886.

And it was on October 16, 1887, that Mathilde Freud was born. Mathilde was the first of six children for Sigmund and Martha. On the evening of her birth, Sigmund had gazed down at his tiny daughter. He stared at her clenched, rosy fingers and at her fuzz of brown hair. Then he had turned lovingly to his wife. "Josef will be proud," Sigmund whispered to Martha, "that we have named

Mathilde after Frau Breuer. I have just written, Marty, to your family. I told them how magnificent you were and how our little daughter seems to feel quite at home."

"We have made her welcome," Martha whispered back from the bed, sleepily closing her eyes. Sigmund tiptoed from the room and walked down the hallway toward the small office where he treated patients. Books lined the walls, and his desk was covered with the neat piles of paper he was using for a new translation on hypnotism and for a work of his own on the anatomy of the brain.

He sat down in his desk chair, feeling tired and dazed. Were fathers, he wondered wryly, supposed to be weary at the birth of a child? Before him was the pad of his daily notes on his patients. Two had arrived that afternoon—a matron unable to sleep because of itching in her legs, and a man who could not urinate unless he lay on his side. Neither patient showed any organic disease, and both had dragged from doctor to doctor, seeking a cure.

Sometimes Sigmund felt a helplessness toward certain of his patients. For the neurotics, who functioned poorly with fears that seemed triggered by faulty cells, the usual prescriptions of massages, rest cures, or hot baths had often failed. Microscopic cell studies did not reveal neurotic illness, but the symptoms and suffering were acute.

Bending forward, Sigmund opened the top drawer of his desk. Inside the drawer was the monograph which he had read—after his return from Paris—to the Vienna Medical Society. The monograph, entitled "On Male Hysteria," had presented Charcot's opinion that hysteria was not just a female disease. But in reading the paper before the society, Sigmund was nearly expelled from the meeting. "How totally *absurd*, Herr Doktor Freud," one neurologist had said. "The word 'hysteria' comes—does it not?—from 'hysteron,' the Greek word for the female womb. Hysteria cannot, therefore, be a male disorder!" And Dr. Meynert, the brain anatomist at the Psychiatric Clinic, had dared Sigmund to produce a single case of male hysteria.

Satisfying Dr. Meynert had been a frustrating task. Physicians at the General Hospital had refused to release either of the two males that Sigmund diagnosed as hysterics. No efforts at persuasion could convince the staff. The doctors, Sigmund realized, were alarmed by Charcot's challenge to established medical theory.

Finally, Sigmund had produced a male hysteric from outside the hospital. The patient's vision had been strangely blurred after a violent quarrel with his brother, and as always the necessary cell damage could not be found. The audience at the Medical Society had observed Sigmund's demonstration and had read his tests and reports, but they did not applaud. Not only was the subject of male hysteria dismissed, but Dr. Meynert also kept Sigmund from using the anatomy laboratory for further research.

Quietly, Sigmund unwrapped a paper-covered cigar. Martha would chide him, he told himself, smiling, for the smoking that filled their apartment with fumes—but perhaps she would forgive him on this night of their daughter's birth. Lighting the cigar from his oil lamp, he sealed the letter to Martha's family. With it, he put another note he had written to a new friend from Berlin, a Dr. Wilhelm Fliess.

One day, Sigmund thought, he would visit Dr.

Fliess in Berlin. And he would go to England, to spend time with his half brothers Emmanuel and Philipp, and with his nephew John. Ever since Paris, he had had a thirst for viewing the world. His fear of the trains had not smothered him, and he would enjoy traveling to Rome. He would see the ruins of the Coliseum and Michelangelo's sculpture. At the Louvre in Paris, he had been lost for hours over the ancient relics, fascinated by the historic past.

Of course, Sigmund reminded himself, the dreams of travel must be postponed. Only several weeks before, when his practice was empty of patients, he had been forced to pawn his gold watch in order to pay the rent on the apartment.

Rising from the desk chair, his dark eyes ringed red with fatigue, Sigmund heard a sudden knocking at the outside door to his office. Who, he wondered, at such an hour? His sister Mitzi, with congratulations about Mathilde? His sister Pauli, growing slender and quick-witted in her mid-twenties? Or perhaps Ernst Fleischl, unable to sleep and in torture from his hand?

Hurrying to the door, Sigmund unfastened the metal lock. Too much noise might awaken the baby or Martha. "Herr Doktor Freud?" came a faltering voice. "I am sorry to disturb you. I did not know where . . . I am . . . feeling so ill."

In the entryway stood a young woman in a green taffeta gown, her hair hanging askew at her shoulders. She did not carry a shawl or a purse, and her breathing was labored. "Come in, come in," Sigmund said at once, and he led the woman to a nearby chair.

"Your name, Herr Doktor, was printed at the

door," the woman stammered. "My friends have spoken of you. I was at a party with my husband. I have not been feeling well . . . not well. I began choking . . . as if hands were about my throat, choking me. I could not breathe. I had to run from the room. I could not stop myself. I am so embarrassed, Herr Doktor! My husband will be humiliated."

The young woman dissolved in tears, and Sigmund took a handkerchief from his pocket. "Here," he said gently. "Dry your tears. Try and calm yourself. How long have you been troubled by this choking?"

"For a whole year, Herr Doktor," the young woman said. "I have been examined, and I am told that I suffer from a weak brain or from imagination. But my throat closes, Herr Doktor! I do not imagine or pretend! I nearly choke to death! It is a miracle that I am still alive!"

Sigmund listened to his visitor describing her symptoms. Hysteria, he thought—the mysterious, undiscovered lesion hidden in the brain. He would ask the young woman to make an appointment for a physical examination. But he was almost certain that the examinations would not show the cause for her hysteria. Had the cause for hysteria *ever* been shown?

How would he help this woman? Sigmund wondered. What help could there be? Even hypnosis was only temporary. He lifted an electric machine from a table and placed it beside the chair. The machine had never impressed him, but it was part of his neurological equipment. "An electric treatment," Sigmund explained to the woman, "will send a slight wave of heat into your nerves and muscles. The heat may relax you, if you care to try it."

Instantly, the woman accepted, and Sigmund attached two electrodes to the sides of her head. He straightened the wires on the machine and told the woman to close her eyes. Then he pressed the round tip of a metal switch. "We will begin," Sigmund had said.

With a buzzing sound, the machine rattled and quivered. The wires were taut with the electric current, but as the woman sat in the chair, Sigmund found himself asking questions about the length of her marriage.

"We were wed a year ago, Herr Doktor," the young woman said.

"About the time, then," Sigmund asked slowly, "that your symptoms occurred?"

Startled, his visitor had opened her eyes and glanced up at him. "Why, yes," she answered. "I suppose that is true."

A flow of energy, a vibration—yet not from the machine—hovered suddenly within the room. For Sigmund, more questions were forming, and he wanted to ask them, wanted somehow to fit the answers together as if they were pieces of a gigantic puzzle. He reached across the machine, and although the woman did not notice, he turned off the switch. "I hope I do not upset you," he said to the woman, "but your husband—is he a kind and generous man?"

"Oh, yes, Herr Doktor," the young woman answered. "He is a banker. He is well respected by the community."

"The community," Sigmund replied, "may

have considered the outside and not the inside. Do you also feel such respect toward your husband?"

His visitor's hand flew to her throat. A gasp sounded, and she was breathless, then, and choking. "I—I do not know, Herr Doktor, what you mean. My husband and I have a . . . successful . . . marriage. Quite successful. Why do you ask? What—"

Sigmund was silent, and his question hung in the darkened air. Then another gasp from the woman gave way to a torrent of tears, and she buried her face in Sigmund's handkerchief. "I have confided in no one," she sobbed. "I am terribly unhappy, Herr Doktor! My husband treats me as a servant. I am afraid to complain. My family is content with the marriage."

Sigmund nodded, watching the points of flame leap at the dome of his oil lamp. "Your husband demeans you," Sigmund repeated, "by treating you as a servant. Do you feel unimportant or perhaps worthless?"

"Yes, oh yes, Herr Doktor," came the muffled answer between sobs.

"But you do not complain," Sigmund continued, surprised at his own rush of thought. "Perhaps it is your illness, then, that complains *for you?* You mentioned that you fled from a party and that your leaving will humiliate your husband. Are you not angry over the way you are treated? Do you not think that your husband deserves this humiliation?"

The young woman wiped her eyes, watching Sigmund as he removed the forgotten electrodes from her head. "Why, yes," she whispered more calmly. "I *have* been angry. But I am also afraid. Do you think, Herr Doktor, that a wife is justified in being so angry against her husband?"

"If you were told such a story about two people," Sigmund answered, "what would you advise?"

The young woman stood up, her breathing less rapid. "I would advise," she said hesitantly, "that the wife decide whether to remain married. And I would advise that she might speak to her husband of her distress."

"Wise counsel," Sigmund had said. "You seem, now, to be feeling better."

"Why, yes—I do," the young woman replied. "What a marvelous *machine*, Herr Doktor! Your electricity is painless, isn't it? I must come soon for another treatment. I do not choke at all! My throat has never eased so quickly!"

Sigmund suggested that his unexpected visitor return on the following morning. But as he ushered her from his office, Sigmund did not choose to disclose when he had switched off the machine, when the current had ceased to flow. He did not share this fact with the woman because other questions were crashing at him like a tidal wave upon the shore. What a strange turn of events, he thought giddily, what an exciting exchange. The young woman, this stranger in his office, had "talked away" her own choking by expressing feelings about her husband! Like Anna O. herself, the woman had swept aside her "disease." What might she have revealed, Sigmund wondered, under the trance of hypnosis; what else would she have said? Perhaps hypnosis could be used to *ask questions* and not only to give commands. But was Charcot mistaken? Had medical science been misled? Could hysteria be caused by the *emotions* in one's mind and not by *physical trauma?*

Sigmund turned down the hallway that would lead him back toward Martha and to his rosy-hued child. Tired though he was, however, he knew that he would not spend the night sleeping. His daughter, Mathilde, had just been born—yet so had a new and extravagant idea. What if, he asked himself, the injury or lesion behind a great portion of Nervous Disease lay in the mind's emotions? What if the body and mind did not exist in such separate realms?

Yes, the theory did seem unscientific. And science believed only in what could be measured or weighed. But *what if, what if, what if,* Sigmund asked. What if the very content of the mind—the half-hidden fears, the wishes, the guilts and regrets—could wield the power and the influence to *make the body ill?*

VI

Exploration

A small but steady stream of patients began to fill Sigmund's waiting room. It was said that Herr Doktor Freud used hypnosis on nervous ailments, even though most doctors warned in horror against it. And it was said that Herr Doktor Freud asked "embarrassing questions" and that a lady should be cautious before stepping into his office. But some of Sigmund's patients talked of their freedom from torment and pain. They had allowed themselves to be led into the strange, hypnotic sleep. During treatment, their breathing and pulse rates had slowed, and they remembered little of what Herr Doktor asked—but often they felt better.

The plaques made by Frau Breuer had been renailed on an apartment at Berggasse 19. In the five years since Mathilde's birth, two sons were born to Sigmund and Martha, and the family had moved to larger but still modest quarters. Oliver Cromwell Freud was born in 1891 and was named after the English statesman, one of Sigmund's childhood heroes. Jean Martin Freud had been born in 1889 and was named after Charcot.

In his new office on the ground floor of Berggasse 19, Sigmund placed a horsehair sofa for his patients, a chair for himself, and several cabinets for his beginning collection of relics. At the foot of the sofa was an old porcelain stove, its logs crackling through the winter as they sent a glow over Sigmund's books. While Martha dusted the furniture or shook the blanket rug on the couch, Sigmund might relate the history of each vase, statue, or bowl that he'd bought—with a few extra savings—from a cluttered shop in Vienna.

"The past, Marty, is alive in all of us," Sigmund would say. "I have discovered this fact in my patients as well as in any Greek bowl."

Three years before, Sigmund had managed a short trip to the town of Nancy in France, where he'd heard that clinic patients were treated by hypnotic suggestion. He had studied the notes on more than ten thousand cases, comparing the results in Nancy and in Paris with his own work in Vienna. Hypnosis was sometimes successful in treating Nervous Disease, yet symptoms could reoccur when a trance had been lifted. Still, the method was useful. In Vienna, Sigmund had hypnotized a country woman who suffered from severe anxiety or fear. He'd suggested that the woman speak to him, while hypnotized, of her most smothering terrors—and the talking had greatly relieved her.

But it was a young English governess named

Lucy Reynolds who had convinced Sigmund of the bond between mind and body. Miss Lucy, a pale and pleasant young woman, had complained of being possessed by the odor of burning pastry. Her examination did not show tumors or enlarged arteries of the brain—yet the odor haunted the young governess night and day.

"Can you help me, Herr Doktor?" Miss Lucy had moaned. "Please, please, I can no longer bear it! The odor never lessens! My nose runs, and my head is clogged. I will do anything!"

Staring into the governess's eyes and speaking to her of sleep, Sigmund had put Miss Lucy into a light hypnotic trance. The young woman lay, unmoving, on the horsehair sofa, her hands folded over her dress. Haltingly, however, she could answer questions. And gradually, Lucy Reynolds had told Sigmund that she was secretly in love with her widowed employer, a man who did not share her affections. And she said that on the day when she had considered returning to England, a tray of pastry was actually baking in the widower's oven.

"Fräulein," Sigmund had asked, pressing carefully forward on this unfamiliar ground, "what did you feel about going back to England?"

Miss Lucy's eyes were half closed. She had sighed deeply and turned her head. "I thought that I should give notice to my employer," the governess answered slowly. "He does not love me. But I knew that I would never again see him. . . . I could not decide. I left the pastry too long in the oven. . . . It burned to a crisp."

His own pulse rate quickening, Sigmund had opened the curtains at the window. He asked his patient to awaken when he next called her name. And then he said to her, "After the pastry burned, Fräulein, you set aside any decision about returning to England?"

"Yes, Herr Doktor," the governess replied. "I scoured the pastry tray until it was shining."

When Miss Lucy awakened, Sigmund explained to her that she had admitted her feelings of love. "Are you embarrassed," Sigmund asked, "at having a desire to physically love?"

The young woman blushed. In nineteenth century Vienna, to even hint at sexual desire was considered indecent. A gentleman would not so much as steal a glance at a lady's ankle. "It seemed improper, Herr Doktor," Miss Lucy said shakily, "to love someone of a higher station. I did not want to possess such unbearable feelings."

"So you were possessed, instead," Sigmund told her, "by the odor of burning pastry. The pastry burned on the day when you were deciding whether to leave the employ of the man you love. The odor possessed you as a substitute for your decision."

"How strange," the governess answered. "Do you mean that I am ill from a desire of the heart? Am I ill from a lack of courage? How, then, shall I recover?"

"Perhaps, Fräulein," Sigmund said, "when you realize that your love is not shameful, you will no longer be 'possessed.' "

With the case of Lucy Reynolds, Sigmund became far more than a practicing neurologist. He was a doctor who had set foot on Josef's "dark continent"—into the mysterious world within the mind. Emotional illness, he believed, might well be a compromise made by the patient against "unbearable feelings." And Miss Lucy's recovery would seem to depend not only on her facing the pain of her feelings, but also on her acceptance of certain feelings inside herself.

Mind linked to body? A sickness of the soul affecting the flesh? In a notebook, Sigmund wrote that unbearable feelings, hidden away and festering like a pus-filled sore, did not simply disappear. Through an indirect route—through the "compromise" of neurosis or hysteria—they could be expressed in physical symptoms, obsessions, and terrors. Or feelings might be displayed through insanity, or *psychosis*—an almost total withdrawal from the world.

On a rare holiday with Martha and the children, Sigmund had climbed the dry, winding trails of Semmering, a mountain resort near Vienna, and his notebook was carried with him. He hunted mushrooms for Martha to cook, but his thoughts were hunting direction. At home, he spoke again to Josef of Anna O. "Your patient, Josef," he said, "developed symptoms after caring for her dying father. Her *emotions* had overcome her—not any physical disorder! The case should be published."

"Not yet, Sigmund," his friend answered. "Not even in light of your extraordinary theory."

"But why, Josef?" Sigmund asked.

"A trivial matter," Josef replied, "but upsetting to my wife. When I was dismissing Anna O. as a patient, she began writhing on her bed. She sank into a fantasy that she was about to bear my child. She had informed the servants. I might have lost my practice to scandal. I left her house at once and have not treated her since."

"The hysteria was not cured," Sigmund said quietly, recalling one of his own patients who had flung her arms about his neck. Perhaps, he thought, an hysterical or neurotic patient felt an unusually deep attachment toward the doctor who gave treatment.

Sigmund continued to experiment with hypnosis. If there were no evidence of organic disease—no brain inflammation, for example, or abscess or tumor; no syphillis, delirium tremens from alcoholism, sclerotic condition, or meningitis—he treated the illness as a neurosis. He had begun using the term "neurosis" to refer to the general area of emotional disorders. Many of the matrons who sat in his office were suffering from sexual neuroses, from guilts over their own bodily pleasures. Yet their prim and proper upbringings had prevented them from discussing or even thinking of such matters.

In one case, a "multiple sclerosis" patient turned out not to have multiple sclerosis. The woman revealed, when hypnotized, that she had once been raped, had become pregnant, and was aborted. It was the woman's feeling of shame that had caused her variety of crippling symptoms. And another patient described hysterical attacks of spitting. Under hypnosis she was able to admit that, as a child, she had guiltily envied the genitals of her little brother, wanting them for herself.

Guilts, rages, and fears—the hidden fuels of emotional illness—were muttered and mumbled to Sigmund during hypnotic trances. After the feelings were given voice, the neurosis was sometimes eased. But Sigmund was disturbed that hypnotized patients did not know, when awakened, what they had just "confessed." And he found that not all of his patients could be guided into a trance. A young woman named Fräulein Elisabeth von Reichardt had never responded to hypnosis. Dragging her legs as she walked and crippled with pain, Fräulein Elizabeth had come each day to Berggasse 19 weeping over a "ruined life."

"I shall never be well," Fräulein Elisabeth had cried. "I shall never be married. Who could want me as a cripple?"

Sigmund had attempted to hypnotize Fräulein Elisabeth, suggesting in a calm, methodical tone that she was growing tired and would sleep. But his patient kept resolutely opening her eyes. "I am *not* asleep, Herr Doktor," Fräulein Elisabeth would say. "I am not the least bit tired. I am wide awake."

After eight sessions, Sigmund dispensed with any efforts at hypnosis. Instead, he experimented with simply asking Fräulein Elisabeth to talk to him and to bring forth any new memories of her past. When his patient claimed that she had already told Sigmund *everything*, he pressed his hands on her forehead and assured her that there was more to remember.

Days went by of Fräulein Elisabeth weeping on the sofa, struggling to capture her fragments of memory. She spoke frequently of a sister who had died and of the coffin at the funeral. "I looked down at my sister's face," Fräulein Elisabeth had said. "And she was beautiful, Herr Doktor."

"What did you think as you looked at your sister?" Sigmund had asked.

"I honestly don't remember, Herr Doktor. I thought— Well, I thought— I thought *nothing.*"

"But surely," Sigmund said, "at such a moment, Fräulein, you must have thought something."

"Nothing! Nothing!" Fräulein Elisabeth had suddenly shrieked, sitting upright on the sofa. *"I thought nothing!"*

For agonizing months, Fräulein Elisabeth resisted the memories of her past, and her resistance stood like a wall inside Sigmund's office. Fräulein Elisabeth herself was helpless against it. Only with tolerance and understanding was Sigmund able to chisel a crack in the wall and to let through the gush of his patient's memories: *"I wanted my sister's husband!"* Fräulein Elisabeth had finally cried. "I saw my sister, Herr Doktor, in the coffin—and she was dead, and I thought, *'Now I can have her husband! Now he can be mine!'* Oh, my poor sister! How could I ever have had such feelings? I can't bear to remember! I will never forgive myself!"

"But, Fräulein," Sigmund said. "All of us may have desires without turning them into deeds. While your sister was alive, you respected her marriage. You made no advances toward her husband. The proof of your moral character, Fräulein, is that your feelings have made you ill!"

In his notebook, while Fräulein Elisabeth improved, Sigmund wrote that neurotic patients resisted knowing what gave them pain. And he saw that what he was unearthing in his office might loosen the chains of neurosis. He must publish what he had discovered. He must share what he'd witnessed of the strange furies in the mind and of their effect upon comfort and health. Spending part of his weekends with his parents, sisters, and brother— and nightly suppers with Martha and the children—Sigmund was, nevertheless, consumed by his work.

He thought constantly of Fräulein Elisabeth's wall of resistance. He had cracked through that wall without hypnosis! And he thought of how Fräulein Elisabeth's memories had been imprisoned behind her wall, locked somewhere within her mind. Her memories were not in consciousness, not in a state of awareness. They had been buried in some secret sort of mental ceremony, lost from awareness but not truly gone.

Yet *what*, Sigmund wondered, was that hidden place in the mind—that place which swallowed the unbearable feelings? Had hypnosis stumbled upon truths by skirting the wall of consciousness? Did human beings possess both a *Conscious* and an *Unconscious*—two separate areas of mental response?

At night, rereading his notebook, Sigmund would pace the floor of his office. "Aren't you coming to bed, Sigmund?" Martha would ask, but he would answer, "No, no, Marty, I cannot." And hours later, he might be circling the living room. One rainy night, he set out across the neighborhood, passing along the slumbering Danube and in front of the shuttered tobacco shop where he bought his daily cigars.

The stretch of Vienna's streets seemed to clear his confusion. Man, he realized, had been said to

have control over his own mind. Generations had
believed in man's total knowledge of inner thought.
And even if a few philosophers—Socrates or Spinoza—had imagined a region of thought beyond
the ordinary, who had listened or agreed?

An "unconscious mind" would *not* be in man's
control. It would be a "place" that, unknown to
man, could store the discarded or painful past, that
could harbor the most shameful of feelings. It would
be a place that could throttle the body into illness,
that would be as deep as the bottomless forest. In
mental asylums were patients who had been shut
away as meaningless souls. Would exploring their
Unconscious lead such patients from darkness?
Would exposing that darkness to knowledge bring
a light that could make them whole?

At home, Sigmund had fallen fitfully into bed,
with Martha sleeping beside him. His questions
were endless. Since he was a child, his questions
had been endless. Fondly, he listened to the
rhythmic tempo of his wife's breathing. She was a
creature of clarity in his life, of stability and peace.
Yet even as he lay close to her, Sigmund felt as if he
were standing on the edge of a huge precipice,
armed against a fortress of old and time-worn beliefs
with only the strength of an idea. He might find it
more difficult to tear down that fortress—*to suggest
that man was unaware of the mind's real structure*—
than he would in pulling, barehanded, the bricks,
stone, and iron from the buildings on the
Berggasse.

VII

The Unbearable Feelings

The household at Berggasse 19 was managed on a strict schedule. The family had grown to include six offspring—Mathilde, Martin, Oliver; and another son and two daughters, Ernst, Sophie, and Anna. Martha had hired a nursemaid, the custom among even the poorer families. And Martha's sister, Minna, had come to live permanently with the Freuds. She was a bright and cheerful companion, even though she had lost a fiancé to tuberculosis.

At exactly one o'clock each midday, Sigmund would enter the dining room for *Mittagessen*, or lunch. Often, he brought to the table one of the relics from his cabinets, speaking to the children of its heritage and beauty. On Saturday evenings, after a full week of work, he allowed himself his favorite card game, *tarock*, with a group of old friends. And on Sunday afternoons, he went without fail to visit his parents. He carried with him, as he had long ago from Kahlenberg Mountain, a bouquet of flowers for his mother.

In the summers, in spite of the cost, Martha, Minna, and the children were sent to vacation in the suburbs, escaping the heat of Vienna. Though Sigmund's leisure hours were scheduled and scarce, he was an adoring father. By August, he would join the family at some vine-covered cottage, marching on his mushroom hunts with the children and tossing a tyrolean cap over clumps of the finer specimens.

When Mathilde had lain ill with diphtheria, Sigmund had not left her bedside. The disease, unable to be medically cured at the time, usually ended in death through a choking membrane in the throat. As his eldest child had weakened, Sigmund promised her that he would grant any wish possible. "Is there anything you'd like, Mathilde?" Sigmund had asked in anguish. "Anything special that your papa can bring you?"

Mathilde had faintly smiled. "Yes, Papa," she'd rasped, her throat thick with the membrane. "Strawberries. I would like strawberries."

The fruit was not in season, but Sigmund had rushed to hire a carriage, a two-horse *fiakur* that he could scarcely afford. He scoured the city, searching from fruit store to market, until he had bought— with relief—several baskets of the plump, ripened fruit. At Mathilde's bed, with Martha standing nearby, he had slipped one strawberry gently in his daughter's mouth.

"*Danke*, Papa," Mathilde had groaned. But as she'd swallowed, the child began to choke so strenuously on the berry that it seemed she might die at once. Only at the moment of turning blue, her eyes rolling upward, did Mathilde dislodge the strawberry from her throat. And with it, freeing her to breathe, had come the gray, sickly membrane of the dreaded diphtheria! The strawberry had accomplished the impossible, and Mathilde would be well—thanks partly to the love and devotion of her father.

Away from family and friends, however, Sigmund was plunging more deeply into the mysteries of the mind. His convictions had been strengthened. He was sending most of his patients with organic disease to other physicians and mainly treating neurotics.

The webs of neurosis were not easy to unweave. There were, of course, the quick recoveries. Healthier patients could be taught new patterns of response without having to continue treatment. But far more common were the cases that needed weeks, months, or perhaps years of painstaking treatment. Sigmund found that he must train himself to a new role. If he wished his patients to talk, to unburden their feelings without hypnosis, he must permit them to do so. He must not intrude himself on them. His patients should have the freedom to flow into their own thoughts, to enter the deepest and darkest of secrets without his pushing or interrupting. The wanderings of a mind—the recounting of tiny details such as the color of a button or the taste of a meal—were like stepping stones in the forest. Amazingly, among what seemed to be aimless sentences, one stone would follow another, forming a pattern of sense. This flowing of thoughts was called, by Sigmund, "free association."

From the years 1892 to 1896, he was building the foundation of his theories. He traveled alone on this uncharted continent, for there were no guidebooks to mark the paths. No scientist or authority had pointed the way before him or could explain the mental world within man. Sigmund's discipline and commitment were tested to the full. Hour after hour, he listened to the tormented tales of his patients. And scrupulously, diligently, he walked the stepping stones, one by one.

"But Herr Doktor," some of his patients would say, "I did not realize that I *had* such memories!" Or others, raised in the prudery of Viennese society, would murmur, "I did not know myself at all, Herr Doktor. I hid such feelings from even *myself!*" Then Sigmund would see, once again, that there was a wall in the path of memory, blocking the feelings in the Unconscious. A patient might hope desperately to be well, yet unconsciously hide the very feelings that were making him ill!

In the midst of treatment, patients would neglect to appear for appointments or would leave on unexpected trips. They would take to their beds with a hacking cough or break or sprain ankles. When questioned, these patients earnestly explained that they had not "meant to forget," that their trips "could not be avoided," that their coughs "were not an excuse."

Sigmund believed his patients. Consciously, what they said was the truth—as they knew it and felt it. But underneath, unknown to them, was the obvious power of the Unconscious. Hiding from the truth, a patient would unconsciously forget the hour for an appointment. Protecting a neurosis, a patient would unconsciously lower his physical guard and allow himself to fall ill.

Walls against feelings stood as a "resistance" to the free flowing of memory. In 1896, writing a monograph on his unique treatment of neuroses, Sigmund first described his method as "psychoanalysis." "Psyche" was the Greek word for soul or mind, and "analysis" meant the study of a whole by separating it into parts. Sigmund wrote that neurotics had "repressed," or forced down, certain memories into the Unconscious. He said that, in order to be well, a patient must not only remember the painful past, but must also refeel the pain of what had been resisted or repressed.

In his office, he moved his chair behind the head of the sofa so that his patients could speak without feeling watched. Patients were told to disclose any thought in their minds, no matter how silly or shameful it seemed. Sigmund sat attentively in his chair, listening to the tortuous flow and tumble of words. He perceived that his patients—and probably most human beings—could feel opposite emotions toward the same object *at the same time.* Just as he had once both loved and hated his nephew, John, it would be possible to both love *and* hate any person or object.

Sigmund gave the name "ambivalence" to this state of opposite feelings. He was now a man with a new perspective into the mind, and he had put behind him his electric machine, his prescriptions for massage, and even his experiments with hypnosis. His instruments had become the words of his patients, words of emotion from within.

And what *were* most of the unbearable feelings that crept through cracks in his patients' walls? What *was* it that had been hidden by patients in the Unconscious, but which seized them with symptoms of illness? Sigmund's patients whispered to him of their sexual feelings. They confided desires that had not been fulfilled or experiences that had shamed them. "I am afraid to tell you what I felt, Herr Doktor," a patient might say, not knowing that he or she was not the possessor of "evil" thoughts but of common and natural sexual impulses and needs.

At Sigmund's insistence, Josef had finally agreed to publish the case of Anna O. The case was included in a book that Sigmund and Josef wrote, *Studies in Hysteria,* which appeared in 1895. While Viennese society looked upon sex as a forbidden topic, Sigmund had dared to write—in his section of the book—that fears and guilts over sexual feelings might be a cause of hysteria. He shocked the reading public and the critics into pretending to ignore his book. And its publication even alienated his co-author, Josef. Years of friendship between the two men were threatened by the boldness of Sigmund's ideas.

Studies in Hysteria was ignored by the public, but Sigmund himself was met with ridicule and scorn. His comments on sexual matters became rampant rumors on the streets of Vienna. His explanation of the Unconscious was laughed off as a delusion. "The man must be insane!" came the outcry. "He was a hypnotist, and now he is a quack! He fills the heads of women with vulgar thoughts."

Many "proper" families would not allow their wives or daughters to continue treatment at Berggasse 19. "Have the neighbors been unkind, Martha?" Sigmund had asked his wife. "I no longer see them walk with you to the shops. Do you realize, Marty, that you've married a man who could have been a conventional doctor, but who is making your life a difficult chore?"

"The neighbors will walk with me again, Sigmund," Martha had answered. "I need no more in my life than you and the children."

In 1896, at the age of eighty-one, Sigmund's father had suddenly died. Forty years earlier, an angry Jakob exclaimed over some childish naughtiness of his son's that Sigmund would "never amount to anything." Now, across Vienna, the very same pronouncement was being made of Sigmund Freud.

Jakob's death unleashed in Sigmund a lingering grief. His dreams were filled with old memories of Jakob, memories that seemed stitched into some tapestry or design. Ever since he'd cried out as a child at his own nightmares, Sigmund had been intrigued by the act of dreaming. In bookstalls along the Tandlemarkt, Vienna's junk market, were books to translate the "meaning" of any dream. Yet such books were nothing more than tricks of fortune-telling and superstition. No scholar or scientist had considered dreams to be worthy of serious study. Sigmund wondered, however, if a dream might not be a message or clue sent up by the Unconscious.

From his patients, he collected a file of a

thousand nightmares and dreams. He began to record his own dreams in the file. And when the eerie images and symbols were put on paper—images like the monsters from his childhood dream, who'd carried his mother among them—Sigmund was struck by the link between the material of a dream and the hidden wishes of the dreamer. Dreams might be helpful, he thought, in exploring the Unconscious. Even though the conscious, awakened mind appeared to distort a dream's content, not every detail had been distorted—and the message might still be read.

Sigmund would soon begin a book on the analysis of the dream. He would call dreams the "royal road to the Unconscious." And in writing the book, he would use his own dreams to analyze himself! If his patients could grow stronger and healthier by understanding their Unconscious, then why shouldn't he? Hadn't he been depressed over his father's death? Hadn't he been victimized by attacks of dizziness or headaches and by his old fears of the trains?

Sigmund's book on dreams was written during the family holiday of 1899. Intently, he sat before a cottage window in Berchtesgaden, in the Austrian Alps. The blue-tipped mountains stirred him with their lofty grandeur, and the words cascaded from his pen onto the pages of a notebook. Over the past few years, he had written the explanations of so many of his theories. His notebooks teemed with references to the Unconscious, to "resistance," "repression," and "ambivalence," to the sexual nature of neuroses. Now he was to enter the kingdom of dreams. He drew into himself on that summer holiday in Berchtesgaden. Analyzing his own dreams was a disciplined act of the intellect, and of courage. His son Ernst had remarked to the family that "Papa seems, these weeks, as if he is walking in his sleep!"

"Papa is working," Martha had answered. "We must try not to disturb him."

Sigmund's inward journey was revolutionary and extreme. He would thrust away at his own defenses, at those unhealed and hidden sores that kept any man from knowing himself. Although his book of dreams was written in 1899, Sigmund would never entirely cease the search into himself. He would use what he learned of his own pain to better understand human nature—and to better tackle the fortress of outside opinion. He had said that a patient must not only remember but must also relive. Well, now he was to be his own patient—and the rules would apply to himself. He would psychoanalyze his own mind.

He would risk, then, whatever oozed from his own depths, no matter what cost he must pay. He felt both excitement and apprehension. His tools would be turned upon himself. The creator would become the experiment. The scientist, at heart, would record the pulse of his own science.

That summer holiday in Berchtesgaden wound to a close. And Sigmund had written, in the midst of his singular journey, to his friend Wilhelm Fliess in Berlin: "I believe I [have been] in a cocoon—and God knows what kind of beast will creep out."

VIII

Outcast

A cool wind circled the city of Rome, Italy, brushing the fountain sprays into mist. It was August of 1901, and Sigmund had come to view the statue of Michelangelo's Moses in the church at San Pietro. He had traveled to other European cities—but always he had postponed any visit to Rome. Only lately did he recall the vengeance of his old hero Hannibal. Hannibal, the Jew, had once commanded his armies to overtake Rome, but the city stood staunchly against him. And for Sigmund, hadn't Rome become a symbol of all that was impenetrable to Jews?

Now, however, he had conquered his resistance to Rome. In the past four days, he and his brother Alexander had visited the Vatican and had strolled in awe across the Sistine Chapel. Yesterday, they had tossed coins into the fountain of Trevi, and today they stopped in wonderment before the marble statue of Moses.

Slowly, Sigmund's vision traced the curves of the statue. He saw Moses in the throes of a fierce struggle, muscles straining in tune with the mind. He believed that Moses would triumph, would outstrip his burdens, would overcome his fear—

Shaking his head, Sigmund wondered whether that message were truly carved into Michelangelo's masterpiece. Or did he see in the sculpture only what he *wished* to see? He could look at his own responses as if he were removed from body and mind. Inside him now was an awareness of himself that he was never to lose. He was emerging from his three-year-long experiment, from his ordeal by mental fire. His face had tautened and thinned, and his forehead was creased with lines.

His gaze bore into the lines of Moses' face. Evidence showed in the sculpted face, too, of prolonged and painful struggle. "The work is magnificent, isn't it?" he whispered to Alexander.

"Yes, Sigmund," his brother answered. "The work of a genius."

One day, Sigmund would write a book on his interpretation of Moses. But for now, he was drawn back each morning to see the statue in San Pietro. How easy it was to flinch under the demand of those sculpted eyes. Whose eyes did he really see? Professor Brücke's icy stare from his days at the university or his father's unhappy glance?

Sigmund would turn in silence from the majesty of the statue. In his dreams was hidden the meaning of many feelings about his father. And of other feelings toward his mother. He had written of those buried feelings in his published book on dreams—and he knew that he had dug from himself, and from his patients, a core of truth for all men.

His book was entitled *Die Traumdeutung*, or *The Interpretation of Dreams*. On his desk, propped between two Etruscan vases, was his personal copy. The book was, somehow, a part of him—like a section of tissue or bone. Yet over the next year, it would sell no more than two hundred copies. One reviewer would attack the book without ever having read it, and it would be dismissed by the journals as a wicked, outlandish joke.

Sigmund, however, would consider *The Interpretation of Dreams* as his most important piece of writing. The price of his self-analysis had been to expose his emotions in print. What he'd learned of his psyche and of the function of dreams was put to use in his book. Dreams, he had established, were not magical omens. Nor were they senseless hieroglyphics that were painted by the mind. A dream, Sigmund had written, was actually the "disguised fulfillment of a repressed or hidden wish"!

When Sigmund's son Martin reported a dream of climbing a high mountain or when Mathilde dreamed that a boyfriend had moved in with the family, the wishes were quite plain. But even in a more complex dream, a wish lay somewhere within the dream-work. By "fulfilling" a wish or longing, dreams allowed the process of sleep to continue. A nightmare was often a dream that had failed, awakening the sleeper from sleep.

One patient reported to Sigmund that he had dreamed of his only brother's death. "Do you *think*,

Herr Doktor," the patient had asked indignantly, "that I wish my brother *dead*? I love my brother. I would not want any harm to come to him."

"Yes," Sigmund had answered. "I understand. But tell me, what did you feel about your brother when he was born?"

"Do you mean," the patient asked, "when I was just a child?"

"Yes," Sigmund had said, "when you were a child."

"Well," the patient answered, "that was so long ago. I was four years old, Herr Doktor. I suppose I did resent a baby coming into the house. I wished that he . . . would be taken away."

"Or that he might die?" Sigmund asked. "Such a wish must be familiar to many children. We fear that our wishes can make things come true— though, of course, they cannot. We bury the most frightening wishes in a part of our minds. And years later we can dream dreams of what we've wished."

Childhood, Sigmund had found, was the fertile field beneath most neuroses. As his patients let go of their secrets, he saw that their illnesses were rooted in childhood. Somewhere, in the past, was an emotional pain or guilt that the patient had not accepted—and that smoldered still within the Unconscious.

In his own dreams and memories, Sigmund had come upon a forgotten rivalry with his dead brother, Julius. When Julius was born, Sigmund, too, had wished the baby away. And when Julius died, Sigmund had been left with a deep, unde-served guilt—as if his wish itself had caused Julius to disappear.

But what of the childhood feelings toward his mother and father? Sigmund's self-analysis, his psychoanalyzing, had drawn him closer and closer to some unsettling knowledge. At first, he had taken flight, escaping the "beast" that might appear. But then he had followed Charcot's advice to "look, look, and look again." He'd pulled apart the images of his dreams as if he were tearing yarn from a half-knitted garment. His search had been relentless, and he would not forsake it.

And bit by bit, he had stumbled upon the shadows of an unconscious feeling. He had pursued the feeling until it took shape, and to his astonishment he discovered in it a strong childhood yearning for his mother—a romantic, almost sexual yearning. And there had been a *jealousy* of his father. Amalie had "belonged" to his father when Sigmund had wanted her for himself. Yet children, Sigmund told himself, did not feel romantic toward a parent, not even if that parent were of the opposite sex. What a peculiar notion! It was absurd, impossible. . . .

Or was it?

Hadn't Sigmund heard one of his own little sons say of Martha, "Momma is mine! I am going to marry Momma when I grow up!"? And hadn't his youngest daughter, Anna, crawled into his lap to ask, "Do you love me, Papa, better than you love Momma? Do you think I'm pretty?" From a dream fragment, Sigmund had recaptured a childhood memory of watching Amalie undress on a train. Had excitement caused him to cringe in shame and to ever after be so dizzy and frightened of the trains?

Sigmund had questioned his patients as they

lay on his sofa—wondering if they, too, had felt a secret childhood longing for one parent—and, surprisingly, he found that most of them had. In guilt similar to his, their feelings had been repressed. And patients were not alone in this romanticized attachment. Sigmund's friends, when asked, could vaguely admit the same reaction.

Questioning and requestioning, Sigmund had gradually pieced together a pattern of human behavior. As the pattern emerged, he watched his own symptoms fall away. In *The Interpretation of Dreams*, he opposed society's belief that a child was entirely "pure" of the sex instinct until adolescence. Sexuality, Sigmund said, appeared to be present from birth.

Even in an infant's suckling there was a broad, partly sexual pleasure. Each child, Sigmund wrote, must have been born with the stirrings of sexual response. In order to preserve the species, nature would have prepared each human being for the later experience of physical lovemaking. Couldn't a little boy, therefore, learn to feel "romantic" as he cuddled with his mother? And couldn't a daughter respond lovingly to warmth and stroking from her father?

Romantic feelings toward a parent would seem to fade, Sigmund wrote, into an easier affection between the maturing child and the parent. But if guilt was too strong, a child might be so uncomfortable with his longing that he tried to repress it. Sigmund gave the name *Oedipus Complex* to a male child's desire for his mother. It was Oedipus, from Sophocles' drama *Oedipus Rex*, who had murdered his father and married his mother—living out, Sigmund realized, a most violent form of the romantic desire. And wasn't it Sigmund's own Oedipal guilt that always brought Amalie and not Martha the bouquets of Sunday flowers?

Many of Sigmund's patients had never outgrown their Oedipal feelings. Rejection or abandonment by a parent, or the neurotic needs of a parent, might keep a person dependent on Oedipal feelings. A child might grow into adulthood and still feel, unconsciously, that he or she should be punished for the early longing. When repressed feelings did not *stay* totally repressed, they could exert a lifetime tyranny over the emotions.

Even though *The Interpretation of Dreams* was rejected by the public—shunted aside as was *Studies in Hysteria*—Sigmund wrote three more books by the year 1905. In the *Psychopathology of Everyday Life*, he showed how small slips of behavior and speech were not just accidental. Unconscious feelings, Sigmund wrote, were disclosed by these slips. If a wife claimed that she had "misplaced" a birthday gift from her husband, she might be showing unconscious anger toward her marriage. And if someone mistakenly sent a letter saying "Dear *Fiend*" instead of "Dear *Friend*," the missing "r" might be an unconscious expression of hostility or fear.

Because of the lighter subject matter, the *Psychopathology of Everyday Life* was read with some curiosity in Vienna. People picked up the book to compare notes on their "mistakes." Eventually, errors of speech and behavior would be known as "Freudian slips," but in the meantime Sigmund wrote of other discoveries in *Three Essays on the*

Theory of Sexuality and *Jokes and Their Relation to the Unconscious.*

He spoke, in *Three Essays on the Theory of Sexuality,* of three stages that he'd identified in childhood sexual development. The *Oral* or mouth stage, Sigmund wrote, spanned the first two or three years of life. In the Oral stage, a baby was focusing his sexual pleasures on sucking or eating. At the second or *Anal* stage, however, the child had become intrigued by the functions of his bowels and bladder. He would often use the timing of his "wetting" or "messing" to either please or distress his parents. And in the third or *Genital* stage—entered by the child at the age of four or five—sexual feelings were more centered on the organs of reproduction.

Sigmund explained that the gap between "normal" and "abnormal" behavior was much finer than had been believed. All humans struggled, he said, with painful, destructive feelings. A "normal" person was not totally free of neurotic behavior. A "mentally ill" person was not a worthless or alien being. Many adults had not passed smoothly, in childhood, from one stage of development to another. They were partially "fixated" or "stuck" at a certain level of behavior.

Fixated at the Oral, or mouth stage, adults might overeat, overdrink, smoke heavily, or be non-stop talkers. Fixated at the Anal stage, they could seem stingy, stubborn, or overly neat or messy. And if, like a newborn infant, they had not yet learned to love anyone but themselves, they might display an obsessive self-love—called "narcissism" after Narcissus, the youth in Greek mythology who fell in love with his own reflection.

As Sigmund worked and wrote past the turn of the nineteenth century, his theories of human nature were forming into a solid base. Yet he was not surprised to find that the resistance he fought in his patients was matched by a resistance outside his office. He was to suffer the same scorn that had been heaped, throughout history, upon so many creators. *Three Essays on the Theory of Sexuality* was met with horror and shock. Society's fortress had been armed against Sigmund's concept of neurosis, and it was better armed against his theory of childhood sexuality. Outraged citizens shrieked that "the madman Freud"—the "depraved, obscene doctor at Berggasse 19"—was trying to destroy the innocence of childhood. The reaction to Sigmund was so heated that his name was no longer mentioned aloud in public if ladies were present.

The waiting room at Berggasse 19 had emptied of patients, and Sigmund's bills were left unpaid. Colleagues crossed the streets in order to avoid him. Perhaps, Sigmund thought, he had asked too much of society. Perhaps he had reached too far. But, for him, seeking the truths of the mind would outweigh any rewards of the safe, dependable life.

Stoically, he said to Martha of his books that, "after all, one doesn't write for today only." And to shield her, he spoke little of his dwindling income or of his isolation within his office. He wrote and he studied, and he treated the few patients who had remained with him. To them, as they were released by psychoanalysis from the traps of their emotions, Herr Doktor Sigmund Freud was far more hero than madman.

Sigmund's closest confidant in his years of isolation was Wilhelm Fliess in Berlin. In letters to Fliess, Sigmund had spoken of being cast like Robinson Crusoe upon a deserted island. Yet even at his gloomiest, Sigmund's mission was pulling him onward. "I am pretty well alone," he wrote to Fliess, "in tackling the neuroses. They regard me as a monomaniac . . ." But then he added that his work with the Unconscious had given him the distinct feeling of encountering "one of the great secrets of Nature."

Fliess had respected Sigmund's work and avidly answered the letters. And although the isolation in Vienna continued, a faint flurry over psychoanalysis began at the university and in medical circles. A letter or two arrived weekly at Berggasse 19, inquiring about the new science. And a few more stacks of Sigmund's books had sold at the shops. As a kind of underground interest, psychoanalysis was discussed during intermissions at philosophy lectures and seminars.

On an October afternoon, a physician named Wilhelm Stekel had actually appeared at Sigmund's office, conferring with him for several hours. Was it possible, Sigmund wondered, that this unfamiliar Viennese doctor could accept the theory of the Unconscious or of childhood sexuality? The answer from Wilhelm Stekel had been emphatically *yes*.

At the General Hospital, Sigmund still held the privilege of lecturing as a *privatdocent*, and he decided to offer a short series of talks on his new "Science of the Mind." Only three or four men gathered, at first, in the huge hospital amphitheater, but by the end of the series Sigmund faced a small group of listeners in a circular row of chairs.

Eagerly, he had mounted the lecture podium. He felt cleansed and inspired as he had felt in San Pietro before the marble statue of Moses. "You will find, gentlemen," he had commented with a slightly shy smile, "that I have had the good fortune to merely discover the obvious. I have studied what every nursemaid must already know: that children have sexual feelings and that dreams have meaning."

Beneath the podium sat a man named Rudolph Reitler, the first physician who would practice psychoanalysis after Sigmund himself. In the adjoining seat was Alfred Adler, the doctor who spoke of "inferiority feelings" in man and who would one day begin the Adlerian school of psychology. Later, the group was to be joined by Otto Rank, a young, poor, but ingenious student; Max Graf, a scholar who taught music at the Conservatory; a Dr. Paul Federn; and then Hanns Sachs, the lawyer who would tell Sigmund that "your book on dream interpretation has changed my life."

The damp, dimly lit amphitheater was suddenly crackling with an exchange of ideas. Psychoanalysis, Sigmund sensed, seemed to be existing on its own. If he set it afloat in the waters before him, he believed that it would sustain itself. The siege on society's fortress might not have to be made alone. When the lecture series was over, Sigmund was encouraged to continue the meetings— and he invited the men to appear at his home on Wednesday evenings. Soon, he was heading what one of the men called the *Psychological Wednesday Society*.

In his lifetime, Sigmund's discoveries about the

mind were never to be smoothly embraced by the world outside. Yet their truths possessed the power to penetrate resistance. Like Copernicus, who reasoned that the earth was not the center of the universe—and like Darwin, who had spoken of man's evolution as being joined to that of animals—Sigmund was a pioneer in his own time. He had forged a pathway that would not close.

From childhood, he had wrestled with fears and uncertainties within himself. He had yearned for strength and for valor, for understanding and knowledge, for the link between causes and their effects. Now, in his middle years, he was in touch with some of the answers to his deeper questions about man. And he had stepped, bravely, into his own forest. Ceaselessly, he had uttered the word *"Why?"* and he was always to utter it. But if no one else attempted a reply or reason—if no one else delved beneath the surface of human nature—Sigmund looked to himself to provide the answers.

IX

The Cause

The chestnut tree was bare in the small courtyard at Berggasse 19 when Sigmund rented three extra rooms. His new office would be located across the hallway from the apartment, but a connecting door was constructed so that he might pass in privacy from one side to another. The children had been growing quickly past childhood. Mathilde had married at the age of twenty-one, and Sophie was engaged. Martin had studied law, Oliver was to be a mathematical engineer, and Ernst was fascinated by architecture. Anna, the youngest, was a dark-haired girl in her teens and had drawn closest to her father.

Sigmund treated patients in his office from eight in the morning until the midday meal at one. Each patient was allotted fifty-five minutes, with a brief five-minute rest for Sigmund between sessions. After lunch, he walked to buy his daily cigars—a straight-backed, pensive-looking man, dressed in a dark suit, with his hair graying at the temples. At three o'clock, his afternoon scheduled with several patients, he would turn back up the steep tree-lined hill of the Berggasse.

The evening meal was spent catching up on the family activities, but after everyone else had retired, Sigmund went again to his office. There, he worked over his latest manuscripts, reread notes on his cases, or wrote letters to colleagues and friends. He had joined a Jewish organization, the B'nai B'rith, even though he had never followed the traditions of Judaism. But he felt a certain allegiance to these men who accepted him warmly, unafraid of his ideas.

Patients had arrived more frequently since the lectures at the General Hospital. Although his name was still food for scandal, Sigmund had been granted the title of Associate Professor when a wealthy patient had influenced the Minister of Education. He could now be addressed as Herr Professor Freud, the title offsetting some of the furor against him.

So his waiting room was less deserted, and he had mailed off the final payment on his old debt to Josef Breuer. Since *Studies in Hysteria*, he had rarely seen Josef or Mathilde Breuer. The years had separated the former friends as sharply as had Sigmund's theories. Yet it was Josef who had said, "You will never, Sigmund, completely abandon science. You will find the road for return." And hadn't psychoanalysis been the delicate joining of medicine to science?

In Sigmund's office, patients were slowly learning to cast an eye inward, to focus upon the self. What Sigmund wanted from his patients was to be told not only what they knew of themselves and had concealed—but also what they did *not* know, what was hidden within the Unconscious. "Listen to everything that is said twice," he had written, "and to that which is never said at all."

Day after day, he saw how guilt over sexual feelings could crush and enslave the spirit. A twenty-four-year-old patient had huddled in Sigmund's office after falsely confessing to police that he'd committed every major crime in the newspapers. The young man's family was horrified, while the patient could only cry out in despair, "What am I to *do*, Herr Professor? I *feel* guilty, even when I know I am not!"

The young man's "crime," Sigmund discovered, was that as a curious and excited child he'd twice watched his parents in lovemaking. Guiltily, the patient had repressed all memories of the scene, and his confessions to the police were his way of seeking punishment. "You will learn," Sigmund had gently reassured the young man, "that sexual excitement and curiosity are perfectly normal in childhood."

Another patient of Sigmund's, a thin, unmarried woman of thirty, could not stop herself from counting objects. The woman had refused to lie down on the sofa, and she stood before Sigmund's cabinets, numbering his antique bottles and vases. "Wherever I go, Herr Professor," the woman had said, "I start up my counting. I count my steps on the pavement. I count the streetlamps at curbs. I count the stained glass windows on churches, and the arabesques that decorate buildings. Why do I do such a thing? How shall I be cured?"

"You have taken the first step, Fräulein," Sigmund had replied, "by seeking to understand."

After three months of treatment, Sigmund's patient had uncovered a desperate loneliness and had admitted her wish for a physical relationship with a man. The counting had been an unconscious attempt to blot out her desires. "But I should not feel guilty, should I," the woman had asked, "for wanting to be loved?"

Sigmund had answered firmly. "All human beings," he'd told his patient, "need to love, and to be loved."

Some of Sigmund's cases were discussed among the members at the Psychological Wednesday Society. Yet honoring the trust of his patients, Sigmund had carefully disguised any names. He published several case histories only after the treatments had long been terminated. His published monograph, "Fragment of an Analysis of a Case of Hysteria," had involved a patient whom Sigmund called "Dora" and whose illness he analyzed through two of her dreams. And a second published case—nicknamed "Little Hans"—described the successful psychoanalysis of a child. A quarter of a century later, when Sigmund's writing filled over twenty-three volumes, the case of "Little Hans" would be a classic in the field of psychiatry.

Five-year-old "Little Hans," considered a hopeless imbecile by doctors who'd treated him, had shown symptoms of terror upon leaving his home. The child insisted that he would be bitten or mauled by a horse, and he screamed in panic on the streets. "Take me home, take me home!" Hans would cry at his parents. "A horse will bite off my leg! Save me, Mama! Save me, Papa!"

Using the father as a go-between in treatment, Sigmund had been able to analyze the child's terror and to uncover deep Oedipal feelings. When "Little Hans" expressed some of his unconscious anger toward his father, the fear of horses had disappeared.

After the case of "Little Hans" was published, many Viennese doctors predicted that the child would be mentally scarred by psychoanalysis and would continue to live a demented life. Yet fourteen years later, a handsome and successful young man had called upon Sigmund at Berggasse 19. "I am little Hans," the young man was to say. "I owe you a great debt, Herr Professor Freud."

Those who had written to Berggasse 19 about psychoanalysis, or who gathered to study the new medical science, had also recognized a debt to their professor. The starkness of Sigmund's total isolation was put behind him. The Psychological Wednesday Society was meeting in larger quarters and had renamed itself the *Vienna Psychoanalytic Society*. And in Zurich, Switzerland, the famous Psychiatric Clinic had been using Sigmund's methods of treatment on patients and was teaching psychoanalysis to visiting doctors. Letters had been delivered to Berggasse 19 from a Dr. Ernest Jones of England, a Dr. Karl Abraham of Germany, and a Dr. A. A. Brill of the United States. All three men were to become Sigmund's lifelong friends. Ernest Jones would eventually write a three-volume biography of Sigmund, while A. A. Brill would translate Sigmund's books into English and practice as the first American psychoanalyst.

In 1907, a thirty-two-year-old psychiatrist from the Zurich Clinic traveled to Vienna to meet Sigmund Freud. The man, Dr. Carl Gustav Jung, was a tall and impressive figure with steel-rimmed glasses and closely cropped hair. Jung was the author of a book called *The Psychology of Dementia Praecox* (a mental disorder later known as schizophrenia), and his first conversation with Sigmund extended for thirteen hours.

The two men were to form a close but ill-fated alliance. Sigmund had been hearing less frequently from Wilhelm Fliess, who had accused his old friend of reading thoughts into patients, and Jung appeared as the bright sun on the horizon. One of the few Christians to commit himself to psychoanalysis, Carl Jung had said to Sigmund, "You have not only created, Herr Professor, a new treatment for mental illness—but your science of human nature can be applied to all areas of man's life."

When Carl Jung suggested an annual meeting for the followers of psychoanalysis, a hall in Salzburg, Austria, was rented for April 26, 1908. On that balmy April Sunday, forty-two men gathered at the Hotel Bristol to hear nine papers on the subject of mental disturbance. Sigmund had sat at the head of a long wooden table. Looking out at the luminaries from Austria, Germany, Hungary, England, Switzerland, and America, he felt that, for him, the day was an unrepressed dream come true.

He had read the opening paper in a strong and

confident tone. He spoke of a severely disturbed patient who had been obsessed by the idea of cutting his own throat with a razor and whose fantasies of rats had been a shield against sexual feelings. Sigmund described his patient's improvement, brought about by eleven months of intense psychoanalysis. "Remarkable!" one of the men at the table exclaimed. "A remarkable case!"

"This patient," Sigmund had said, "has not entirely erased his conflicts. However, we learn that human beings thrive on a certain amount of conflict. We do not suggest trying to remove all obstacles or stress."

The international congresses began to meet nearly every year. Psychoanalysis, with its unique perspective of the mind, was building into a scientific movement or cause—and some of its followers referred to the movement as *"die Sache"* or "the Cause." The first publication devoted to psychoanalytic writings was sponsored by the International Psychoanalytic Association, and at the Psychiatric Clinic in Zurich a *Yearbook* on psychoanalysis was published. Sigmund asked Carl Jung to be editor of the *Yearbook* and to serve as head of the association. Jung's presence, Sigmund felt, might put an end to accusations that psychoanalysis was a "Jewish science." Articles against the Jews had been appearing from Germany, and Sigmund had hoped that Jung could sway German opinion.

After the second congress, however, Sigmund was approached by his Viennese group. Some of the members were bitterly resentful of Jung's position in "die Sache." Jung was the "foreigner," Sigmund was told. Had "the Swiss" been a part of the original society—of that small band of listeners who'd dared defend Sigmund Freud? Why did Sigmund choose to favor him over everyone else?

Alfred Adler, the doctor who wrote of man's feelings of inferiority, was especially irate over Jung's rise in the movement. Ambitious and outspoken, Adler had once snapped at Sigmund, "Do you think, Freud, that I want to spend my whole life standing in your shadow?"

Were men always, Sigmund wondered, to resort to their childlike jealousies? Alfred Adler would break away from the Vienna society, taking eight other men with him and denouncing any emphasis on the Oedipus Complex or the Unconscious. Turning more fervently to Jung, Sigmund was unaware that Carl Jung, too, would balk at sharing the leadership.

Sidestepping any mention of sex, Jung's lectures in Switzerland quietly departed from the basic foundations of psychoanalysis. Yet the proofs of psychoanalytic theory had been shown in patients from Zurich, as well as from Vienna. Where was Jung's commitment to childhood sexuality, repression, and resistance? Where was the agreement that a child's sexual and emotional development could influence his or her adult experiences in society?

The relationship between Carl Jung and Sigmund was not to be saved. Jung would leave "die Sache" in 1914, forming his own practice of "Analytic Psychology." Partly in reaction, Sigmund would then write *The History of the Psychoanalytic Movement*, a detailed explanation of psychoanalysis. Before the final break, however, both men were invited to speak on psychoanalysis at Clark University in America. Word of Herr Professor Freud's method had apparently spread across the Atlantic, leading Sigmund to remark that he must be showing enough gray hair to qualify as an "aging revolutionary."

Excited by the invitation to America, Sigmund, Carl Jung, and a psychiatrist friend from Budapest, Sandor Ferenczi, had sailed in 1909 for Worcester, Massachusetts. On shipboard, Sigmund realized for the first time that he was gaining popular fame. Walking across the deck, he had seen a cabin steward deeply engrossed in a book. Printed across the book's cover was the title: *Psychopathology of Everyday Life.*

Using no note cards, Sigmund had spoken at Clark University in his native tongue of German. The reaction to his talk was a mixture of criticism and praise, but he knew he'd gained a few followers from a foreign shore. His audience was filled with collegiate men and women, and their shiny, up-turned faces had made Sigmund acutely aware of his own age. Time had slid by so stealthily, and he was in his fifty-fourth year. On a tour of Niagara Falls, he'd been jarred by the words of the tour guide who'd held back some of the crowds for him. "Let the old fellow pass through," the tour guide had said, and Sigmund had winced at the casual comment.

In 1913, Sigmund found a publisher for a new volume of his work, *Totem and Taboo.* In this startling book, having studied early religion and mythology, Sigmund offered a psychoanalytic view of the origins of religion. Tracing religion back to primitive

tribes, he suggested that an "Oedipal murder" may
have been committed by tribesmen against their
leader or "father." In guilt, the tribesmen might
have substituted a totem animal for the dead
"father," setting up taboos about killing or eating it.
Religion, Sigmund had written, was a type of obses-
sional neurosis.

As furious as religious scholars were over *Totem
and Taboo,* psychoanalysis was sending down roots
into the hard ground of medicine. For every inch
gained by "die Sache," however, society's fortress
reassembled its weapons. In London, Ernest Jones
was asked to resign from a neurological post because he supported psychoanalysis. In Budapest,
Sandor Ferenczi had been reminded that "Freud's
work is filth," and was prevented by the Medical
Society from publishing a paper on Freudian theory.
And in Berlin, any institution that tolerated Sigmund's work was threatened by boycott.

Yet no mob would decide on the right or wrong
of psychoanalysis. Sigmund had withstood the
heaviest artillery of world opinion. If supporters
deserted him, he had nurtured his ability to gather
strength from distress. His office, its window fram-
ing a lone chestnut tree in the courtyard, was a
sanctuary where he tested and retested his theories.
He had watched the healthy and unhealthy forces
of personality waging their war against each other.
And he had come to believe that although the
voice of reason might speak, at times, in a whisper,
it would someday be heard above the chaos and
darkness.

Outside, across the arcades and boulevards of
Vienna, a darkness was threatening in the rumbles

of actual war. The solitude of Sigmund's study was broken by the shouts of newsboys who ran up and down the Berggasse. Headlines suddenly blazed from the *Neue Freie Presse*, announcing that the Crown Prince of Austria had been killed by a fanatic in Serbia. And later editions of the paper told of Austria's declaration of war against Serbia and of the mobilization of Russia. "What will become of our sons, Sigmund?" Martha had asked. "Will they be forced to leave us and take arms?"

"I am presuming," Sigmund had answered grimly, "that the people will come to their senses." But he had gone, then, to stock his mother's kitchen with food and supplies. And it was not long before Germany had declared war on Russia, England was at war with Germany, and World War I—the 1914 war that was known as "the war of all wars"—had thunderously begun.

Untamed and unthinking, the furies from the Unconscious had torn through walls of resistance. Hatred and greed had swept across cities and towns. Sigmund could visualize the whole world in a struggle of reason against madness, of creation against destruction. War had loosened those savage impulses that mankind tried to control. In war, human beings were pitted against human beings—as well as against themselves—and war within became war without.

With his shelves of books stretching behind him, Sigmund had stood at an open window above the courtyard at Berggasse 19. A warm July breeze was playing lightly over the lace curtains, but the floor planks of his office were shifting from the roar of a distant cannon. Yet weren't human beings, Sigmund had asked himself, too basically rational to keep on repeating the past without *ever* learning from it? Wouldn't the voice of reason be ultimately heard?

X

A Tide Turns

Vienna no longer sparkled with its style of measured gaiety. Traveling musicians and peddlers had disappeared from the parks, and in coffee houses—where businessmen stopped to buy foreign newspapers or talk over a cup of coffee—the tables were dust-streaked and bare. The "war of all wars" had been taking its toll. By 1918, Austria-Hungary, Germany, Turkey, and Bulgaria, calling themselves the Central Powers, were quivering in defeat against the Allies—France, Great Britain, Belgium, Russia, Italy, and finally the United States. Seven million young men had been killed in battle; eighteen million more were wounded or maimed.

Sigmund's three sons had fought in World War I, much to the family's anguish. Martin wrote home that bullets had ripped through his cap and sleeve. Then he dropped from sight to recover in an Italian hospital from wounds. Others close to the Freuds had been tragically killed. Sigmund's sister Rosa had lost her son, and Emmanuel, Sigmund's half brother, was crushed in a wrecked train. A few of Sigmund's old teachers and friends—tumor-ravaged Ernst Fleischl and Professors Brücke and Meynert—had died of old age or illness. Death, it seemed, was stalking the world.

"We have a dark time in front of us," Sigmund wrote of the war, "which impoverishes us as much in spirit as in material goods." "Die Sache" was nearly torn asunder by World War I. Colleagues and disciples were drafted for service, and the *Yearbook* stopped publication. The annual congresses were postponed, and patients were drifting out of treatment. Little time or money was left for neuroses.

In Vienna, food and fuel had become dangerously scarce. The green and yellow tile stoves were empty of logs, and inflation was ruining the economy. A whole suitcase of inflated Viennese kronen bought one loaf of bread. With a handful of vegetables, Martha cooked large pots of soup that she spooned out over a week. Her dresses sagged at the waist, and her face was sunken and drawn. "You must rest, Marty," Sigmund told her. "You should be out in the fresh air."

But Martha had busied herself with her housework. Smiling fondly at her husband, she answered, "Outside, Sigmund, there are starving dogs who beg for food we cannot spare."

Over a long clutch of months, Sigmund treated only two patients—an American and an Englishman—and they were sent to him by Ernest Jones. In the biting chill of his office, he and his patients wore heavy overcoats and scarves. But even in the frigid hours of the late evenings, Sigmund settled back at his desk. His teeth chattered in the cold, and his fingers grew numb, but by candlelight he had written a monograph on what he called "transference." He described "transference" as an unconscious process in which patients relive and understand their painful relationships by "transferring" the emotions of those relationships onto the doctor. If a patient believed that he suffered from a cruel parent, he might act angry or hurt at the psychoanalyst, as if the analyst *were* the parent.

The war was to deeply affect the future of psychoanalysis. The battlefield had left its emotional scars on thousands of soldiers. Physicians were overwhelmed by the cases that they could not cure. Words that Sigmund had used in his books began to be repeated by other doctors—words like "anxiety," "male hysteria," "ambivalence," and "repression." From Chile, a Spanish physician wrote that he was practicing Sigmund's method. And from India, an English doctor said that psychoanalysis allowed his Mohammedan patients to interpret their childhood memories. Old textbooks were laid aside, and old treatments were being discarded. The new "cure of the soul"— Freud's psychoanalysis—carried sudden authority.

In Budapest and Berlin, clinics were opened to treat war neuroses. Cases that had been exposed to psychoanalysis were making improvement. The few analysts employed by these clinics had been trained by Sigmund as "lay analysts." They were men without medical degrees who possessed the skills and techniques for analysis and who treated patients under the guidance of doctors. Both Hanns Sachs and Otto Rank had been trained for such work.

In Vienna, however, psychoanalysis was barred from the clinics. Not even as the war halted—with the Austro-Hungarian Empire split by Hungary's claim to freedom—did Vienna unbend very far toward Herr Professor Sigmund Freud. For fifty-eight years, Sigmund had made his home in the golden city by the Danube. He had probed more deeply into man's inner world than had any thinker before him, and he had unearthed a structure in himself, and in his patients, that appeared true for all men. But the Vienna Medical Society still held him at arm's length.

At a family reunion in Salzburg, Amalie had celebrated her eighty-second birthday. The deadly roar of the cannons was silenced, and the Freud sons had returned from battle. Amalie beamed at Sigmund's every gesture—for her, the Oedipal "romance" had never ended. Sigmund, however, was gripped by an aching weariness. Was it the war, he wondered, that had been so depleting? He drew his family more closely around him. There was much for which he was grateful. Martin, Oliver, and Ernst were healthy and safe. A savings account had been opened for "die Sache" by a wealthy young friend, and plans were under way for new congresses and for an independent publishing house, to be named the Internationaler Psychoanalytischer Verlag. His office was graced by world-famous callers—by H. G. Wells, the English novelist, and by Count Hermann Keyserling, the German philosopher.

Yet the reunion in Salzburg would be the last happy holiday for all of Sigmund's offspring. In the aftermath of the war, cities were mending across Austria, Hungary, and Germany, but without warning an epidemic of influenza had struck down Sigmund's daughter Sophie. Married and the mother of two children, the lovely Sophie had died within days of falling ill. Her death, so stinging and unexpected, had taken Sophie in the bloom of her twenty-seventh year. She was just "blown away," Sigmund had uttered in sorrow and disbelief.

Martha was stricken with such grief over Sophie's death that she was put to bed by her sister Minna. In his own weariness and loss, Sigmund had immersed himself in work. By 1923, he had added to his dream theories, stating that dreams not only satisfied hidden wishes, but could also frighten or "punish" the dreamer in order to satisfy guilt. He also explored further into his concept of the mind's structure, producing a major book that he called *The Ego and the Id*.

Enlarging his theory of the Conscious and the Unconscious, Sigmund divided the mind into three main areas of mental response. He described the *Id* as the seat of man's most unconscious and primitive urges, as that darkest cave in the mental forest where passions could seethe uncontrolled. The Id did not deal, Sigmund said, in reasonable thought. It boiled with the primal urges of "I want!" or "I need!"

The *Ego*, in contrast to the Id, was said to think rationally and to solve problems. The civilized Ego could deal with the world outside, and could set up a wall against the Id. And the Ego could draw upon some of the primitive impulses from the Id, harnessing them in a useful force. This harnessing, or change, was called "sublimation." Sigmund believed that the great works of civilization were the result of primitive urges being "sublimated" from the Id.

Sigmund called the third area of the mind the *Super-Ego*. Like a judge in a court trial, the Super-Ego announced its verdicts or decrees. Formed from the rules of parents and authority figures, the Super-Ego was the inward voice that said, "You must!" or "You must not!"; "You are good!" or "You are bad!"

"Psychoanalysis," Sigmund wrote, "is the instrument to enable the ego to achieve a progressive conquest of the id." For many patients, a balance had been lost between the Id, the Ego, and the Super-Ego. A weak Ego might allow the Id to run wild, as in criminal behavior. And an overly strict Super-Ego might cause a person to punish himself with guilts, fears, obsessions, accidents, or failures.

The Ego, the Id, and the Super-Ego could be locked in a furious struggle for power. Sometimes a weak Ego was unwilling to admit its fear of the Id's desires. The Ego might attach its fear onto outside objects, as in phobias of crowds, heights, and open spaces.

At Sigmund's sixty-seventh birthday, a few of his books—and many of his more than seventy monographs—were being printed in foreign languages. Patients were seeking psychoanalysis in major cities around the world. Popular magazines from America were dabbling in the strange terms, Ego, Id, and Super-Ego, and at the University of London a lecture series was offered on five Jewish philosophers: Philo, Maimonides, Einstein, Spinoza, and Sigmund Freud. While Vienna kept Sigmund at bay, the International Psychoanalytic Association could boast two hundred and thirty-nine members. Various thinkers had awakened to the magnitude of Sigmund's theories, and scholars were applying insights from psychoanalysis to other fields of study.

The tide was turning permanently for "die Sache," but Sigmund could not shake off a lingering weariness. Even a full night's sleep would not erase his fatigue. The war and Sophie's death had gravely affected him, but he harbored a deeper loss that he did not understand. A vigor had left him, and he thought of his long-finished visit to America and of the tour guide at Niagara Falls who had called him an "old fellow."

On a morning in April, 1923, Sigmund had sat at the dining table at Berggasse 19. He was eating a slice of bread when he noticed a fresh spot of blood across the buttered crust. Stiffly, he'd risen from the table to walk toward a mirror in the lavatory. A few years before, when cigars were scarce in Vienna, a sore had chafed inside his cheek. But a new box of cigars had arrived in the mail, and after he'd inhaled the smoky fragrance—it was sweeter to him than the scent of jasmine in the parks—the sore had soon disappeared.

Sigmund stood now in the lavatory and stretched back his cheek with one finger. Blood oozed over his nail, and he saw that the sore had returned. A leap of anxiety tumbled in him, but then he shook his head at his own foolishness. Quickly, he washed his hands in the sink. "Herr Professor," he spoke in amusement to himself, "you have, I believe, a touch of hysteria."

The sore, however, did not heal. In mid-April, Sigmund forced himself to consult a surgeon, a Dr. Hajek, who examined the cheek under a magnifying glass and a lamp. "There is a small growth, Herr Professor," Dr. Hajek had said. "It does not look serious. We can remove it, at your convenience, in the out-patient clinic."

Near the front desk, Sigmund signed an appointment book for the morning of April 20. He did not mention the growth to Martha or to the rest of the family. He occupied his leisure hours by answering each of the letters that were delivered daily to Berggasse 19. Friends and strangers were writing to him, and to some of them he spoke of an increasing concern for civilization. To the French author Romaine Rolland, he'd said, "If in the course of evolution we don't learn to divert our instincts from destroying our own kind, if we continue to hate one another for minor differences and kill each other for petty gain, if we go on exploiting the great progress made in the control of natural resources for our mutual destruction, what kind of future lies in store for us?"

On the morning of April 20, Sigmund walked to the out-patient clinic at the General Hospital. He was dressed in a black suit and tie, his beard having been trimmed by a barber, and he approached a waiting bench with three other patients. Almost at once, however, a nurse came to escort him into a square whitewashed room. He was well known enough, it appeared, to receive immediate service. He was seated in a wooden chair, a bowl positioned next to him in which he would spit his blood.

The sunlight was fanning through a leaded window as Dr. Hajek greeted him. "Good morning, Herr Professor," the doctor had said, and with a signal to the nurse, he sprayed Sigmund's cheek with cocaine. Again, this drug that had caused addiction was put to good use. Sigmund steadied his hands in his lap, fixing his concentration upon a tray of instruments. "Now, Herr Professor," Dr. Hajek had said, "keep your mouth open as wide as possible. Try not to move."

Silence had hung in a canopy over the room, and then a gleaming scalpel had swept into Sigmund's mouth. There was a throb of thick and unyielding pain. Sigmund saw that Dr. Hajek was frowning, and he braced himself against the scalpel that cut at his cheek in weird spirals and circles, like the swing of a baton. Tightly, he'd closed his eyes. His stomach was churning, and his head reeled with a dizziness. Somehow, to be dizzy was an old and comforting symptom.

When a quarter of an hour had passed, Sigmund was drenched with perspiration. What was happening? he wondered. What was the delay? If the growth were as harmless as had been thought, he should have been strolling home by now to treat his two morning cases. He opened his eyes, and suddenly—with a tearing sound from his mouth—he felt blood gushing into his throat. *"Don't swallow! Lower your head!"* Dr. Hajek commanded. *"Spit into the bowl, Herr Professor!"*

Gasping, Sigmund had lurched forward, emptying his mouth of blood. The scalpel pursued him, however, and in fifteen minutes more the final chunks of the growth dripped on a fold of white towel. Sigmund's cheek was packed with gauze, and Dr. Hajek wiped hastily at the stains on his patient's suit. "We had some difficulty, Herr Professor," Dr. Hajek remarked flatly. "I must insist that you remain overnight in the hospital. We have a vacant bed alongside another patient. May I phone your family and ask them to bring you a change of suit?"

Sigmund could do nothing but mutely nod. Martha would be alarmed to hear that he was in the hospital, but he had not thought it necessary to prepare her. He let himself be guided down a hallway to a thin metal bed in a tiny room. On another mattress, he saw a severely deformed male, dwarfed in appearance, who grinned blankly up at him. Trembling, he sank onto the bedsheets, wondering if he might be having some sort of nightmare that he must analyze when he awoke.

Martha and his daughter Anna had rushed from the Berggasse to the clinic, their faces stricken with fear. "I am quite well," he told them, but they sat numbly in the visiting chairs until a nurse asked that they leave during the luncheon meal. Nodding good-bye, Sigmund had rolled, then, onto his side, the dwarf muttering at him from the other bed. A train whistle had sounded beyond the window, echoing a much older but resolved terror. Drowsily, he'd heard the clatter of lunch trays in the corridor. He turned his head on the pillow, but the packing in his cheek must have instantly frayed. He felt something drop down onto his tongue, and again his mouth was filling with blood.

Gagging, Sigmund reached upward for the bell

at the wall. His cheek, however, was hemorrhaging so rapidly that he could neither call out nor press the bell. Would he die? he thought dizzily. Was the end truly upon him? He coughed torrents of blood onto the bed. Feeling himself grow cold and lightheaded, he could not lift an arm and could barely draw a breath. He was drowning alone in a sea of crimson.

Only in half-awareness did Sigmund glimpse the bent and dwarfed figure of his roommate limping grotesquely across the floor. *"Help! Help him! Bleeding!"* a voice had rasped into the hallway. And only vaguely did he sense the commotion of nurses and doctors or the hypodermic needle in his arm or the heavy new packing lodged in his mouth. He was not even certain, in the following days, whether he ever thanked the twisted little man who had saved him from death.

His cheek wound slowly healed, and Sigmund had come home to Berggasse 19. Dr. Hajek informed him that the growth in his cheek was benign—that it was not cancer—but Sigmund's intelligence could not be misled. He would not speak of the surgery. When Anna changed his dressings, he talked with her of the books and journals that she had been reading on psychoanalysis.

Each morning, as was his habit, he unlocked his doors for his patients. "What have you been thinking?" he would ask them as they stretched out on the sofa. His attention was given to the abounding of words and to that laboratory that was the *mind*. He sorted out the stepping stones in his patients' memories, connecting one stone to another until the forest pathway was firm and complete.

Thus Sigmund spent his convalescence from

the removal of the growth in his mouth. His surgery was to be the first of thirty-two operations, spaced over sixteen years of a spreading cancer, upon his cheek, mouth, and jaw. He would never be wholly free of the malignancy that had invaded him. Yet Sigmund's mission had long been fused to his ardor for his beloved "science." Not even the chill or the weariness of death could dim such a passion.

XI

Destiny Fulfilled

"For Herr Professor Freud!" the errand boy kept announcing. Sprays of flowers, baskets of fruit, and a flood of telegrams and gifts had been delivered, on May 6, 1931, to Berggasse 19. Sigmund was seventy-five years old. Fame and distinction had suddenly taken residence. Sigmund's birthday was noted in cities in Europe and America, and the Czechoslovakian government held a celebration in his honor. In Freiberg, the town of his birth, a plaque was nailed on the old whitewashed house in which he'd been a child, and even in Vienna a small token was bestowed. The Vienna Medical Society, which once laughed at Sigmund Freud for describing male hysteria, had elected him a member.

Turning down any birthday invitations from friends, Sigmund had celebrated the day with his

family. Only one visitor was permitted in the afternoon, a former patient who was quite devoted to
the Freuds, the Princess Marie Bonaparte of
Greece. Over cups of hot tea, Sigmund had shared
stories with the Princess about a small chow dog
she'd given him. One of the dog's puppies was
Sigmund's constant companion. The puppy had
been named Lün and was a great comfort to its
master.

Sigmund marked his seventy-fifth birthday
with calm. Amalie had died the year before, and he
was partially relieved that, at the age of ninety-
five, his mother did not have to cope with the
creeping sickness in his mouth. On Sigmund's
seventieth birthday, Amalie had traveled with a
cane from a nearby suburb, arriving at dawn as his
first visitor. "A man who has been the undisputed
favorite of his mother," Sigmund had said,
"keeps for life the feeling of a conqueror, the con-
fidence that often brings real success."

And new successes had come to Sigmund. In
Frankfurt, Germany, his writing style had won him
the Goethe Prize for Literature. Goethe's essay on
Nature had first inspired Sigmund to explore the
glories of science, yet he was too ill to appear at the
awards ceremony. For the League of Nations,
however, he'd found the energy to write a series
of essays "Why War?" with the famous physicist
Albert Einstein. And from America, he'd been offered $25,000 from the *Chicago Tribune* if he would
comment on two wealthy young murderers, Leo-
pold and Loeb, who had attempted a "perfect
crime" in the killing of a little boy.

Sigmund had refused the *Tribune*'s offer, just

as he would not accept the $100,000 bid from Samuel Goldwyn, the Hollywood movie director, for advice on a film about sex and love. Psychoanalysis was fast becoming a fad in America, with the Unconscious a topic for cocktail party chatter, but Sigmund was not interested in publicity stunts.

On the evening of his birthday, he unwrapped a large box of cigars. The smoking inflamed his mouth, but he could not seem to give it up. "My favorite neurosis," he would readily admit. At the clinic, his cheek tissue was scraped every two weeks, and in one of his operations a part of his upper right jaw and palate had been sliced away. He had been fitted for a painful mechanical piece that closed off his nasal cavity from his mouth and that he had named "the monster."

The mechanical piece had to be continually reshaped to fit him. "The monster" sometimes clamped Sigmund's jaws so tightly shut that he had to pry them open with a clothespin in order to eat, smoke, or talk.

He lit a cigar now from his lamp and sat wearily at his desk. Behind him, Anna stepped noiselessly across the rug, covering him with a robe. "We're stacking boxes of mail for you, Papa," Anna said. "The errand boy suggests that you have your own private postal station on the Berggasse."

"Too much fuss for a birthday," Sigmund answered his daughter. "There are better accomplishments than the one of growing old."

"But you have those accomplishments, too, Papa," Anna gently replied.

Sigmund had looked up at her with deep affection. It was Anna who had become his nurse and who encouraged Martha not to worry or strain. Anna helped him insert "the monster" into his mouth, and she had agreed to his one request: he would not complain of his discomfort, while she must not express sympathy for him, or pity. The request had been fully met.

Anna was never to marry and would be the sole child of Sigmund's to follow in his footsteps. Anna Freud would contribute her own skill and insight to the medical science of psychoanalysis. She would be the author and editor of books, articles, and journals and would specialize in the treatment of emotionally disturbed children.

In 1930, Sigmund had written of his concern for mankind in a book called *Civilization and Its Discontents.* Unlike his early writing, the book was quite well received. He spoke of the problems of the individual within society, and he had isolated the defenses used by the human personality against these problems. Along with "repression" and "sublimation," Sigmund included "regression," an unconscious return to infantile behavior such as temper tantrums, and "projection," the displacing or shifting of one's feelings onto some other person or object. A man, for example, who felt jealous of his brother might "project" that jealousy onto the brother. The man would argue that he himself felt no jealousy and that it was *his brother* who possessed the feeling.

Sigmund had often explained the human psyche in terms of two opposing forces. He'd talked of the Conscious and the Unconscious, and of the "pleasure principle" of the Id against the "reality principle" of the Ego. After studying the history of man, and in his years of fighting cancer, he also formulated the concept of a "life instinct" and a "death instinct." Human beings, Sigmund said, were pulled by the urge for preserving life and sexuality, and by an opposite urge for self-destruction, aggression, and death. From the Greek language, he used the word *Eros* to symbolize the life instinct and *Thanatos* to describe the impulse toward death.

In his own body, destruction was gaining a firmer hold. Sigmund's speech had slurred from the operations, and although he would not stop treating patients, he greeted them with a hot-water bottle pressed against his neck. To cheer him, some of his patients brought bowls and figurines for his collection of relics, but others were too obsessed by their own symptoms to notice the physical pain on "Herr Professor's" face.

A few patients talked not of their doctor or of themselves, but of the world's newest crisis—of the specter of Thanatos, the death instinct, and of its threat to all Europe. The patients at Berggasse 19 were mostly citizens of Austria, but in nearby Germany was the rise of a Nazi political regime that had been fed on hate and oppression.

Sigmund hoped, as he'd hoped before World War I, that the voice of reason might be heard. But, once more, he was disappointed. A man named Hitler had seized control of Germany, vowing to "cleanse" the nation of Jews. Many Jewish psychoanalysts had fled their homes in May, 1933. In that month, Hitler's Nazi ministers had ordered the burning of over 20,000 books, and among the ashes were the remains of every book available by "that Jew, Freud."

Sigmund's friends began to plead with him to leave Vienna. If Hitler crossed the borders of Germany, if the Nazi menace spread into Austria, the Freud family would be in danger. Yet Sigmund did not want to desert his patients or to part from his surroundings. He was accustomed to working in the same building, on the same street. The Jews, he said, should no longer have to run in fear from persecution. And besides, he was sick and growing very thin. It would take such an effort to leave.

On March 12, 1938, Nazi armies had tramped across the Austrian border, intent on overpowering Europe. Shouts of "Heil, Hitler!" rang out in Vienna, and the Nazi emblem—the swastika—was chalked onto the sides of buildings. Tanks rumbled down boulevards, equipped with guns, and groups of Viennese Jews were robbed of their savings and herded into concentration camps. On March 15, Berggasse 19 was looted by soldiers. A week later, Anna was snatched by the Nazis for a day of abusive questioning.

Ernest Jones had flown at once to Vienna. "You have no choice but to move," Jones had said to Sigmund. "You must think, my friend, of your family—if not of yourself." And Sigmund, who had felt a devastating fear when Anna was missing at Nazi headquarters, had nodded his head.

Special permission was required for any Jew to leave Austria. Ernest Jones spent several months working on Sigmund's release, persuading President Roosevelt of the United States to try and influence Hitler. Herr Professor Freud, Jones had implored the President, belonged to the world. How could any nation not protect this man who had created a whole new science of mental and emotional health?

Weeks dragged by while arrangements were made, and in the meantime the Nazis seized the library at the Vienna Psychoanalytic Society and destroyed the contents at Internationaler Psychoanalytischer Verlag, the publishing house. At last, Hitler agreed to free Sigmund and his immediate family for a ransom of nearly five thousand dollars. No sooner was the ransom announced than it was paid—by the Princess Marie Bonaparte of Greece.

In June, after the older Freud children had fled, a taxi carried Sigmund, Martha, and Anna to South Station in Vienna. The decision had been made for the Freuds to go to England, where Ernest Jones had rented a temporary home. A final order from the Nazis demanded that Herr Professor Freud sign a paper stating that he had been well treated by the police. Sigmund did not realize that millions of Jews would soon die in Nazi incinerators and ovens. And he would never know that the four sisters he left behind—assured by the Nazis of their safety—had been gassed to death in the ovens.

The Freuds traveled out of Vienna on the Orient Express. Sigmund looked gaunt and in pain, but the gaze of his eyes was penetrating and direct. Regardless of the obstacles against him, he had become a monument to the world. The force of his ideas had given him recognition from many sources that once renounced him. He had fulfilled the prophecy of the old peasant woman who'd peeked at Amalie Freud's infant son in a childhood carriage, promising him greatness.

Even though his heart was weakened from the cancer in his body, Sigmund declined a wheelchair at the stopover in Paris. His strength, and his life, were nearly gone, yet he insisted on walking un-aided across the slats of the station platform. "I am again the refugee without a country," he'd said to Martha, pressing her hand. "But if anyone catches sight of me, let them view me on my feet."

Sigmund would be welcomed more warmly in London than in all his years in Vienna. Minna would join the family by late summer, and the rented house would be exchanged for a brick home at 20 Maresfield Gardens, in the city's Hampstead section. Sigmund's books and his furniture, his dog Lün and his collection of relics, were shipped to him from the Berggasse. Martha fretted over his meals, and he finished his last complete manuscript—the study of Michelangelo's statue of Moses. He even accepted a few patients, and al-though he was critically ill, he enjoyed moments of tranquil beauty in the flower garden behind the Maresfield house.

In September of 1939, Sigmund willingly swal-lowed a tablet for pain. Steadfastly, he'd been re-fusing his medication, saying that he preferred "to think in torment" rather than not "to be able to think clearly." But the strings of life were breaking loose, and he remarked, "It is only torture now, and it no longer has any sense."

In the last half of the month, Hanns Sachs came to visit him. There was talk of psychoanalysts needing to be analyzed themselves so that they were not bound by their own neuroses. And the two friends reminisced together over the early, isolated days of the Wednesday Psychological Society. From those days, Alfred Adler and Wilhelm Stekel had both died, and Carl Jung—who'd split so abruptly from "die Sache"—had not refused to work with the Nazis. Sigmund's voice had faded at the mention of Jung's name. "He was lost to us all," Sigmund had whispered to Sachs.

On the twentieth of September, Ernest Jones paid a call at 20 Maresfield Gardens. Sigmund, however, was too ill to speak and had simply raised a hand in greeting. Martha and Anna were hovering in veiled shadow by his side—always, they had comforted him—and Lün was curled in warmth at his pillow.

Sigmund felt himself sinking, then, into a deeper part of the forest—his enchanted, long-ago forest—than he'd ever before seen. It was dark amidst the cloak of trees, and the vines wove around him in a strange and haunting dream. He was not afraid. He was at peace. He knew that his "Cause," his creation named psychoanalysis, had carved a safe harbor onto the shore of ideas.

He let himself sink further, ebb deeper—and on the twenty-third of that September, 1939, his cancer had claimed Sigmund Freud. The world was told that he was dead.

Yet Sigmund had bequeathed to the world a priceless and brilliant gift. From his work and his writing had come a new instrument of observation. Sigmund had found, through *the power of words*, a beam of light into the mind—and if that light limited man's illusions, it also increased man's capacity to understand and to be free.

Because of Sigmund Freud, as the poet W. H. Auden wrote in eulogy, a "whole climate of opinion" was changed. No other thinker in modern times had such a profound effect on so many branches of knowledge. The insights of psychoanalysis would be used in medicine, child care, religion, law, science, anthropology, penology, social work, literature, art, drama, and music. Because of Sigmund Freud, people could communicate with a greater potential for honesty. Children would be considered more often as individuals—not as "miniature adults"—and their impulses, feelings, and self-expression might be explored. Penologists would study the motives of criminals, and penal codes would be revised. And because of Sigmund Freud, human sexuality might one day be discussed without the old rigidities of guilt, shame, and fear.

In the field of art, the "unconscious mind" became an exciting and fertile subject. Painters such as Pablo Picasso and Salvador Dali created luminous symbols to represent the Unconscious. Virginia Woolf, the author, wrote in a new, free-floating style that was called "stream of consciousness"—and in his fictional work *Ulysses*, James Joyce depicted twenty-four hours of thoughts from the Unconscious of one man.

No longer would human emotions be trapped on a dark unexplored continent. No longer would dreams be easily dismissed or the mentally ill classified as completely apart from the "sane." Psychoanalysis had prompted people to confront their deeply buried feelings and to expose the secret and sometimes frightening forces that govern each human being from within. The time-honored cliché "What you don't know can't hurt you!" was proved a lie by Sigmund Freud. Sigmund discovered that "What you don't know *can* hurt you"— that even though the Unconscious may be buried, it is buried alive. Its demons can beset both body and mind.

Today, the acceptance of an Unconscious is so universal that it is hard to comprehend the courage of Sigmund Freud. This man who lived in an age of Victorian arrogance had dared to question what most men held dear—the illusion that they were in total control of their own thoughts. Some of Sigmund's theories are still debated: Is there a "life instinct" and a "death instinct"? Does psychoanalysis overemphasize sexual feelings, or does the emphasis exist because of the basic importance of sexuality?

Much of the debate over psychoanalysis is, in essence, a tribute to Sigmund's greatness. A lasting need has arisen to come to terms with his work. In 1955, ten years after the defeat of Nazism in World War II—and sixteen years after Sigmund's ashes were placed in a Grecian urn in Golder's Green, a suburb of London—Ernest Jones presented a bronze bust of Sigmund to the University of Vienna. Mounted in a courtyard near the austere marble halls where "Herr Professor" had been an outcast, the bust is inscribed with a line from Sophocles' drama *Oedipus Rex*. The line reads: "Who divined the famous riddle and was a man most mighty."

And divining that riddle—the riddle of man—was what had first enticed Sigmund on a journey that reached beyond all confines of ordinary space and time.

Knowledge had been the lure of that fateful journey. Truth was the prize to be won at journey's end. The world has lived and thought differently since the life of Sigmund Freud.

Bibliography

Arlow, Jacob A., M.D. *The Legacy of Sigmund Freud.* New York: International Universities Press, 1956.

Baker, Rachel. *Sigmund Freud.* New York: Julian Messner, 1952.

Barea, Ilsa. *Vienna.* New York: Alfred A. Knopf, 1966.

Brill, A. A., M.D. *Freud's Contribution to Psychiatry.* New York: W. W. Norton & Co., 1944.

Brome, Vincent. *Freud and His Early Circle.* New York: William Morrow & Co., 1968.

Choicy, Maryse. *Sigmund Freud: A New Appraisal.* New York: Philosophical Library, 1963.

Costigan, Giovanni. *Sigmund Freud, A Short Biography.* New York: Macmillan Co., 1965.

D., H. *Tribute to Freud.* New York: Pantheon, 1956.

Erikson, Erik H. *Insight and Responsibility.* New York: W. W. Norton & Co., 1964.

Freud, Ernst L., ed. *Letters of Sigmund Freud.* New York: Basic Books, 1960.

Freud, Ernst L., ed. *The Letters of Sigmund Freud and Arnold Zweig.* Translated by Elaine and William Robson-Scott. New York: Harcourt Brace Jovanovich, 1970.

Freud, Martin. *Sigmund Freud: Man and Father.* New York: Vanguard Press, 1958.

Freud, Sigmund. *An Outline of Psychoanalysis.* Translation by James Strachey. New York: W. W. Norton & Co., 1949.

——. *The Basic Writings of Sigmund Freud.* Translated and edited by A. A. Brill, M.D. New York: The Modern Library, Random House, 1938. (Includes *Psychopathology of Everyday Life, The Interpretation of Dreams, Three Contributions to the Theory of Sex, Wit and Its Relation to the Unconscious, Totem and Taboo, The History of the Psychoanalytic Movement.*)

——. *The Origins of Psychoanalysis, Letters to Wilhelm Fliess.* Edited by Marie Bonaparte, Anna Freud, Ernst Freud. New York: Basic Books, 1954.

Fromm, Erich. *Sigmund Freud's Mission*. New York: Harper & Row, 1959.

Hall, Calvin. *A Primer of Freudian Psychology*. New York: World Publishing Co., 1954.

Hürlimann, Martin. *Vienna*. New York: Viking Press, 1970.

Jastrow, Joseph. *Freud: His Dream and Sex Theories*. New York: Pocket Books, 1969.

Jones, Ernest. *The Life and Work of Sigmund Freud*. Vols. 1, 2, and 3. New York: Basic Books, 1953, 1955, 1957.

Klagsbrun, Francine. *Sigmund Freud*. New York: Franklin Watts, 1967.

Lagache, Daniel. *Psychoanalysis*. New York: Walker & Co., 1963.

Lauzun, Gerald. *Sigmund Freud, The Man and His Theories*. New York: Paul Erikson, 1965.

McGlashan, Agnes M., and Reeve, Christopher J. *Sigmund Freud, Founder of Psychoanalysis*. New York: Praeger Publishers, 1970.

Puner, Helen Walker. *Freud, His Life and His Mind*. New York: Dell Publishing Co., 1947.

Roazen, Paul. *Freud: Political and Social Thought*. New York: Alfred A. Knopf, 1968.

Robert, Marthe. *The Psychoanalytic Revolution*. New York: Harcourt Brace Jovanovich, 1960.

Schoenwald, Richard L. *Freud, The Man and His Mind*. New York: Alfred A. Knopf, 1956.

Stone, Irving. *The Passions of the Mind*. New York: Doubleday & Co., 1971.

Stoutenberg, Adrien, and Baker, Laura Nelson. *Explorer of the Unconscious: Sigmund Freud*. New York: Charles Scribner's Sons, 1965.

Walker, Nigel. *A Short History of Psychotherapy*. New York: Noonday Press, 1957.

Wechsberg, Joseph. *Vienna, My Vienna*. New York: Macmillan Co., 1968.

Wortis, Joseph. *Fragments of an Analysis with Freud*. New York: Charter Books/Bobbs-Merrill Co., 1963.

Index

psychiatric training, 23, 24, 25–27
science, attitude toward, 9, 12–13,
 18–19, 37, 102
Sekundararzt, 25
self-analysis, 65–66, 68
sisters, killed by Nazis, 109
smoking, 41, 56, 80, 97, 105
Sperl Gymnasium, studies at, 1, 5,
 7
travels, 3, 15, 33–34, 49, 52, 59, 65,
 66, 67, 86–87, 109
truth, attitude toward, 7, 9, 75, 78,
 114
University of Vienna, entered, 12
writings, 13–14, 26, 29–30, 40, 63,
 65, 69, 73–74, 82, 86, 87–88, 93,
 95, 96, 104, 106, 110
Freud, Sophie, 58, 79
 death of, 95
Freudian slips, concept of, 73

General Hospital (Allgemaine
 Krankenhaus), 16, 21, 23–24,
 25–27, 41, 98–101
Genital phase, of childhood
 development, 74
Goethe, Wolfgang von, 9, 104
Goldwyn, Samuel, 105
Guilt, feelings of, 47, 53, 63, 70, 72,
 81, 95

Hajek, Dr., 98, 99–100, 101
Hamburg (Germany), 21, 28, 33
Hannibal, 4, 67
"Hans, Little," case of, 82–83
*History of the Psychoanalytic
 Movement, The* (Freud), 86
Hitler, Adolph, 107–108, 109
Hypnotism, 35–36, 46–47, 48, 49, 50,
 53, 54, 56, 60, 62–63
Hysteria, 24, 34–36, 40–41, 43, 52,
 53, 63
 See also Males, hysteria in

Id, concept of, 95
Infantile sexuality, concept of, 71,
 72, 73, 74–75
Inferiority, feelings of (Adler's
 concept), 77, 86
Insane asylums
 Fools' Tower, 23
 Salpêtrière, 34, 36

Insanity, 24, 27
 See also Psychosis
Instincts
 sexual, 72
 See also Life instinct; Death
 instinct
Institute of Physiology, 11, 12,
 13–14, 20
International Congresses, 85, 92, 94
International Psychoanalytic
 Association, 85, 97
*Internationaler Psychoanalytischer
 Verlag*, 94, 109
*Interpretation of Dreams, The (Die
 Traumdeutung)* (Freud), 69

Jealousy, feelings of, 86, 106
Jews. *See* Anti-Semitism
*Jokes and Their Relation to the
 Unconscious* (Freud), 74
Jones, Ernest, 83, 88, 92, 108, 109,
 111
Jung, Carl Gustav, 84, 85–86, 87, 111
 See also Freud, Sigmund,
 desertions by colleagues

Koller, Carl, 31

Lay analysts. *See* Analysts, lay
Leopold-Loeb murder case, 104
Life instinct (*Eros*), concept of, 107,
 113
London (England), 88, 110
Lucy Reynolds, case of, 49–52
Lün (Freud's dog), 104, 110, 111

"Male Hysteria, On" (Freud), 40
Males, hysteria in, 34, 40–41, 103
Memories, repressed, 55, 56, 61, 62,
 81
Mental disorders, early treatment of,
 23–24, 28, 34–35, 41
Mesmer, Franz, 35
 mesmerism, 35
Meynert, Dr. Theodor, 29, 41, 92
Mill, John Stuart, 15
Mind, influence on body, 35, 47, 52,
 56, 57
"Monster, The" (Freud's mouth
 prosthesis), 105
Moses (Michelangelo's sculpture),
 67, 68, 110